HOW TO DO DRAG

Tracy Tramp
My story

All text copyright.

First published April 2021.
v.12 2023

Forward

MY STORIES from a wild period of life in London will not outrank those of *Boswell's London Journal*, though I can see many similarities with Boswell's experiences with my own – and many others. Since Boswell wrote his journal, how many have come to the big city expecting the streets to be paved with gold and shimmering in fame and fortune? Boswell had let-downs, depressions; made friends; felt a bit superior to the Edinburgh set he had escaped from; had fun and frolics and some cerebral activity too – all possible in the big, glamorous stink-hole. I was born in London. I was glad to leave it. Better to go back to a city as a tourist on your own terms, later on, which is more fun – as Boswell eventually realised.

I have a few well-produced books on drag in my collection; some by eminent photographers and journalists. They stitch together interviews interspersed with lengthy commentaries. My time in London was unique and I do not think this will have been written about before in this way; especially due to some of the clubs mentioned which are very 'underground'.

Many people I knew in London pre-millennium – early 2000s had foreign language barriers, or they needed to stay incognito. They could not record much about their fascinating lives apart from blogs, internet title-tattle or unless a journalist tapped them for a photo-shoot or article.

This strange world starts at an early age. It then becomes a lifelong pursuit. There are so many fallacies about it and non-comprehension of it by straight and gay people, despite many prominent TV shows, films and media stunts; it is time to present the story from an insider.

Contents

Chapter 1
Who is who?

These are my own impressions of who is who in the world of drag – built upon my own observations over many years. This will be a handy background read so the rest of the chapters make more sense. Skip and skim it if you like or browse it later.

[Drag Queens/Drag Kings] are predominantly from the gay community – unless they are actors or pantomime dames. Most real drag queens, (who belong to a very small clique in a city or large town), work in gay clubs, bars, at gay or gay friendly events – or even in straight venues. They sometimes have an 'act' of sorts, usually lip-synched material, or they DJ in bars. These types tend to fit most peoples' image of what a drag queen is all about; the Lilly Savage or RuPaul sorts. These queens are also are seen hosting hen-nights or charity events. Some drag queens make it big and get on the telly and achieve stardom.

The next level of this is a little more creative (or at least it is according to its exponents): These are Holly Brubach's 'club-kids'. They have roots (even if they may not know it themselves) going back to the famous clubs of the 1980s and 90s where drag expanded to a wider audience and participants – drag became ultra-creative and intellectual. Outfits made a statement or a constituted a piece of art – chalk to the cheese of the cabaret-style, traditional drag queens who look fab, but in a different way. Of course, each group is rather sniffy about the other and thinks themselves as showing true, pure drag. Some achieve fame and fortune, if they are lucky enough to be in the right place at the right time and look good on the telly.

Many drag-queens, draggoes or 'dress-ups' (as we used to term the whole cadre) also work at 'mix-and-mingle' level in night clubs or do guest lists – standing about by the front door looking fab – or touting outside clubs trying to lure punters in (good example is Canal Street). Others turn up at clubs and dress-up parties for fun or free drinks; or until they get offered work. 'Are you working?' was always a badge of status if you were being paid to be there and dress up. These types are also usually very creative.

The majority are drag queens. I once hooked up with and went about with a lovely drag king, 'V' for a few months. We made a great couple. There have been many books published on the 'drag king' phenomena (before anyone upbraids me on the scant reference). I have little knowledge about that scene though, so I will stick to queens.

Drag queens/kings will most likely have sewing machines and spend all week visiting haberdashery shops, vintage stores, remnant bins and skips and making a new outfit every week for club nights. The objectives are to wow everyone, confuse some, amaze some and irritate other contenders with your fabulousness.

Another echelon of this is best described as 'costume-artistes' or 'dress-ups' but *not at all* like theme park or comic-convention characters. Dress-ups are ultra-creative, very individual and very artistic. For men, this is (sometimes but not always) a sort of 'man-drag' form i.e. not trying to look stereotypically feminine, but with some interesting gear on and powerful, stage make-up – somewhat ambiguous.

Leigh Bowery was the most famous dress-up of them all and made it big-time. When he arrived in London, from Australia, he promised himself that he would wear make-up every day – quite a challenge for a guy then – even if the New Romantics were wearing make-up. Leigh Bowery took creativity to an unsurpassed level and there was not, nor is there now anyone, anywhere who could have ever upstaged him.

There is a big difference between a 'drag queen and a boy in a dress' (*Priscilla, Queen of the Desert*). Any young, skinny guy can put a dress on and look okay, but a drag queen shows heaps more creativity and panache – as they ought to if 'performing' or being paid. A boy in a 'department store dress' will not do professionally.

Drag queens do not get turned on (so they say) by dressing up; they do not revel in wearing silk stockings and panties (as many cross-dressers do). From the stage at Heaven night club, Miss Kimberly, once yelled to all the assemblage of clubbers and queens, "you're just a bunch of ole' trannies" which was funny.

Why be a drag queen? There is obviously something going on with a 'femme' side of many gay guys and vice-a-versa with the girls. For the queens, there is also freedom of expression and achieving a level of glamour and glitz that you cannot (without a lot of agro) as a man. Clothes politics, gay rights, showing off, getting attention are factors too. Drag queens rarely dress for sex unless they are making money out of it. Drag queens (more so in London) can get very bitchy and catty if they think they are being outdone by another queen. A queen once started a fight with me at Heaven club, in the large upstairs toilets, for absolutely no reason at all as I had never said two words to her before.

Drag queens usually have that particular gay intonation of speech and can be very camp. Some gay guys hate 'femmy boys and draggoes'. Some tolerate it. Some love it. Feminists usually hate drag queens as it is a send-up of femininity and female exhibitionism; presenting an even more exaggerated form of it. Names on show bills such as: Millie Mop, Miss-Understood, Betty Swallocks, Betty Swallows, Mandy Gap, Ritzy Crackers, Venus Mantrap say it all.

[Tranny/Transvestite]   The term Tranny is used in the UK. Trannies dress up (in feminine appearance) to different degrees but do not normally do this as paid work (there are a few who would do it for money and that means what you think it means).

'There were a few 'girls' on the street or in the bar when I was there' – is the more usual way of putting it. 'Dressing' seems to be used more now as an interrogative in conversation or even an adjective (dressed). No-one in the UK uses the term 'transvestite' any more. It sounds like a disease and was last heard on the *Rocky Horror Show* (though Eddie Izzard uses it about himself).

[T-girl] This term is now prevalent. T-girls are usually the better presented trannies on the scene. They can be young, but not always; being young is an easy victory in looking great – before the dad-bod happens. Sometimes they have their own hair. Some are fab looking and totally natural. Some 'pass' like a queen I once worked with. She was chatted up on the tube regularly. Small-fine-boned features and a slender body helped. Some look stunning and magically appear in a club or bar, swoosh about pouting at themselves in the mirrors, do some gymnastics on the dance floor and then exit when everyone has seen the show.

[Passing] I was once told I could 'pass' by some T-girls on a night out (at Ron Storme's in Stepney) in the early days. It is quite a compliment. I would have no illusions now. Look stunning whatever you are. They (straight and non-scene people) can usually tell gender (and that is what passing means) the moment they see your face unless you are post-op and very feminine. I have, as I write, read a news article about a trans person getting agro in a straight club in

Manchester (of all cities, really!) from a bouncer. When she opened her mouth (as the voice had not been altered) she suffered some abuse. Any abuse ruins your day, when you thought you were being accepted (whatever level you are at) – nothing changes. The girl said that she had always preferred LGBT spaces, as it was safe. Nothing changes. These days, trannies are accepted in many metropolitan 'normal' places. Some actually delight in going to straight bars, restaurants and shopping centres – possibly more than sticking to the LGBT safe places.

Quite a number of T-girls are wibbling around with hormones, laser hair removal and getting breast implants and other stuff done. Unlike the drag queens, there is a lot more going on with gender fluidity and trans-sexualism in this category as with 'trans', rather than making artistic statements and being an exhibitionist.

[Trans] is another term that embraces the whole sector, though I think that it refers best to those going further with medical procedures.

[Female impersonator] is a term that used to be bandied around but no-one uses that anymore. It could only refer to truly 'convincing' girls. At one time if you were not totally convincing you would be sussed out and could be arrested for female impersonation!

[Convincing] can mean vaguely femme or totally passable depending on whom you talk to. Some use the term on websites and they are only fooling themselves.

T-girls are mainly bi-sexual. Many like playing around with other T-girls. Most want to be 'the woman' with a man.

[Cross-dressing/ers] is a sub-division of the Tranny category and they are usually referred to as Tranny/CDs or use both terms freely about themselves. They are mainly fairly masculine in appearance, voice and gait and usually present as 'a guy in a dress and wig'. They can spend quite a bit of time on make-up and detail but they do not usually rate themselves as 'convincing' or particularly feminine. They are never camp, shrill or noisy exhibitionists.

One night, at the legendary Ron Storme's, I remember chatting to a CD. He was a huge geezer and had hands like shovels; "used to race motorbikes". Now done up in a floral print dress with handbag parked on the seat. He did not look that good (in my conceited opinion), or girly; but had some guts: for a big, rough, geezer to put some slap on, get into a flowery dress, clutch a handbag, paint nails, and go out to be seen and socialise or even present this image to friends and family.

Sometimes CDs have their wigs pulled too far forward giving an odd hairline (often hairdressers mention this) and CDs are rarely fully or even part-shaven; hairy legs showing through three layers of tights. They are usually very nice people, with no malice. They sometimes look uncomfortable in a gay bar – but sometimes gay venues are the only safe places to go to in public where you will not get any hassle or sniggering lads.

Although the better looking girls may sneer a bit, is it up to you what you wear and why should anyone criticise? Many CDs and trannies go out in public big time, such as turning up at Ascot etc. They are not usually the creative drag queen types; most of their wardrobe is womens' wear straight of the rails. In an ideal world anyone should be able to wear what they like and men should be able to have fun with their clothes: wear polka dot fabric, pink scarves and heels – and have the same rights as women – who can be 'masculine' if they want to or keep femininity to the bare minimum.

CDs are usually straight and married with kids. Sometimes they like to play with other T-girls or would like to experiment with that but have not quite got round to it yet. They rarely like men sexually. They sometimes get very affronted if a man makes any approach to them even if they are propping up a bar in a recognised gay venue. Most CDs have a particular look about them and if you are on the scene, you will know. Some CDs let on that they would like to go further down the trans path.

It is sometimes hard to guess exact status unless you talk to someone in detail. So be careful and do not assume. If someone asks you if you are 'full time' (you dress everyday as a lifestyle choice, not only for the night) it can be a bit of compliment as your look is judged to be slick and well finished.

[A guy in a dress] No wig, barely any makeup and to all accounts presenting as a guy in a dress. Some 'girls' denigrate this mode; but, who is anyone of us to criticise? Good luck to him. He is expressing himself and probably challenging gender and clothing norms in a purer fashion than others with silicone-tits, padded hips and voice training. This is why any sub-branch should not be castigated according to a supposedly 'higher' standard. Who of us sets our standards? You? Then you are as bad as the non-trans community for yelling abuse at a man if he is wearing little shorts or a pink scarf. Ultimately, we need to rid ourselves of the male/female distinction in society and officialdom. What does it matter if you are designated M or F. Why does HMRC or your suppliers need to know if someone is a Mr or a Mrs? Just use the name.

[Admirers] Admirers are usually males. They are admirers of Trans/T-girls/CDs and trannies. That means they like them and they want relationships or sex with them. Some only like transsexuals or [she-males] – (used to refer to those in the trans process) and do not go for CDs or even well turned out trannies. Admirers usually have no sexual interest in the camp drag queens or club-creatives. Trannies are not usually camp, but they may get a bit more femme when dressed, you cannot help it sometimes. Clothes do change you. Maybe if we all wore dresses and heels, and were feminised, society would be more peaceful with no wars...but then the Romans wore tunics, so did the Saxons and the Greeks and men used to wear heels with tights. I will back-peddle on that one.

The admirers (who are 99% men, in fact I do not think I have ever met a female admirer) come to the tranny clubs, bars and events. I like them. They make us feel good. They have got some guts, to chat up a T-girl in public.

Girls normally outnumber admirers twenty to one at events or bars. A lot more admirers hide away online. Many have jobs where they would not want it known where they hang out or their preferences. Most of them look so ordinary; you would pass them in the street and not turn a hair. You could say mostly they are bi-sexual. CD/T-girl is the limit of that and they generally do not like 'men' as men. Some of them use T-girls as an excuse to have a homo-erotic experience without feeling so hung up about it as the doll is vaguely or convincingly feminine. Some of them are obsessed with T-girls and prefer them to RGs (real girls).

The terms 'masculine' and 'feminine' are very hard to quantify, but I use them in the sense that most people would understand them or relate to them.

Chapter 2
Drag; when and where?

DRAG IS DIFFICULT during daylight for most of us. It is mainly the cakey make-up – every flaw shows up in the cruel light of day. Unfortunately it does seem as if there is a time and a place for this: nightlife. A drag queen presents an exaggerated form of female-esque high glamour and even females with heavy make-up and OTT outfits look a little out of place in broad daylight. There are trannies who dress full time; some of them are passable in daylight and the look is more girly than drag queen.

At Sparkle† as the day-fun morphs into the night-scene and you have re-touched up late evening, changed and are then out again – being made-up and dressed up seems to become the norm and your drag persona becomes 'normal'. After a few days in a row dressing up and going out and about in Manchester Village or in town, your normal mode of attire with no make-up starts feeling abnormal. It is interesting how quickly norms can be subverted.

You meet some fab people from all walks of life on the scene.

Sparkle, 2019. Pie and a pint in the Goose. The tranny on my table was a prominent player on the 1980s climbing scene...well, well. Another set of in-terms and code-words. Another secret society. Worlds do sometimes collide.

Leeds First Friday. Nearly two hundred T-girls are packing it thick around the Cosmo's brightly lit bar. The bartenders are struggling to keep up. It is a marvel being in a throng (I once contributed to a thread on TV-Chix to describe a collection of T-girls) of make-up, corsets, wigs, heels and handbags, and only one or two biological women to be seen; as friends or wives. (You can spot them, but sometimes you are never sure...). So many T-girls you know or have seen before. I always wonder why there are not five-hundred here as it is such a good event. The biggest tranny event in the North...and where is Eddie Izzard?

Pride weekend. Chicken McNuggets at McDonalds late at night with Lina. We are standing in the queue fully dressed as if it is normal. Hardly anyone turns a hair. A real girl in the queue behind me tells me I have a bit of paper stuck to my shoe (is that some sort of coded message). No one can say anything shite to you on this day, not during Pride. It is a thrill, knowing that I would never dare to do this on any other day (I am a bit of a chicken really); especially McDonalds and in the middle of Leeds. It is only a short hop from the Viaduct and we went back and forth a couple of times for the novelty. It is a great atmosphere, everyone is talkative and in a good mood; our table is busy as we prop ourselves up on high stools and pop nuggets and chips. People come and go. I could almost be back in the Old Compton Café in Soho.

The UK tranny scene is generally like a very friendly club – there are very few bitches, unlike the London 'dress-up' scene which is very competitive and queeny – a total contrast to a night out in the Village. You could spend your life trannying/dragging-up/clubbing around the UK with all the cities and their scenes and all the clubs and parties.

† Once a year event for all trans people in the Village, Manchester. The participants are usually more T-girl than drag queen, but it is open to all of the trans community.

Chapter 3
The Wayout Club.

I ALWAYS WANTED TO DRESS UP. I loved fancy dress. I was always in the school play; any excuse to dress up. I had an interest in clothes, coming from a family in the rag trade (very high class stuff). Dressing up started from about the age of fifteen (some start even younger, especially many trans people). I had nightmares and dreams about being gay but I enjoyed dressing up too much in secret to stop – a common story. I had missed out on the uber-cool, creative generation of Kinky Gerlinky, the Blitz club and meeting all those leading club-land luminaries of that era. I had no idea what was going on in London in the 1980s.

Somehow, a decade later, I found the Transformations shop, then in London. This is where anyone new to the scene and clueless, could start by visiting.

Transformations was a drab 'ole place; a bit like one of those old 'Fashions' shops (they all had that yellow tinted plastic anti-sun-fade-screening over the windows); full of kit your granny would not wear. All big black court shoes or red stilettoes in size tens and everything double the price of a normal shop. (This was before ASOS, internet shopping and TK Maxx). It was a good business at the time and it seems as if it still is. Some of the products (fake body parts) make me a bit queasy, but it takes all sorts... The standard advice from these shops was to 'choose a wig two shades lighter than your own hair colour'. What bollocks! Do women do that? No, they dye their hair outrageous, unnatural shades and mostly go blond if they can. I managed to get a few bits and pieces together, it was very primitive really. It was all so 'naughty', it does give a frisson of pure excitement. It is even more warming when you find out you are not the only one doing it.

Knowing nothing, I drove up to Manchester, to Club Lash. The internet had only started and I was able to get some info, otherwise it would be damn hard: you would have to go and ask everywhere and scan the press for adverts. Later on I did pick up flyers in bars in Soho and found some great parties and one off events to go to and, if the system goes down, we can always go back to that method. There was an elderly tranny who used to come to all the clubs with a home-made, home printed (on an ancient Photostat machine producing that shiny look) – *TV News*. It was good info and a contact point, the only one for many. So many car-shares from military bases were listed..... There were also other orgs, mags and clubs around but I could not find them at the time. There are some tranny organisations with very imperious sounding names...The Beaumont Society (after a notorious tranny diplomat), Northern Concorde...I think one or two still exist. Nobody has ever asked me to join, pshaw! Contact me if you want to advertise your organisation here.

Club Lash was a fetish club. I was not that into fetish itself but it was somewhere to go and trannies are welcome at most fetish clubs, so long as you are dressed up; or if they are fussy, you need to be in rubber or leather – if it is bit purist fetish. Fetish should mean anything that gets you goin'. In most clubs it did but 'street' clothes were always banned. There was always some idiot trying to get in jeans and a T-shirt. Street clothes were okay-ish on a tranny as you were 'dressed' and the 'no denim' rule gradually became relaxed as the tide of the nondescript could not be turned back. My denim hot-pants were an exception to the rule, of course. You could usually change in the toilets. Some had proper dressing rooms. These days most clubs have proper dressing rooms – or it is hard work, or worse if you have to travel dressed – which some enjoy anyway as part of the excitement.

> The drive up...all that fun and excitement building up. Paying a tenner to get in. Picking up the lingo of a secret world... Met some other trannies quickly; birds of a feather; went round with them; K (a hot, curvy dom) getting her tits licked by a posse of trannies. Back in the car, make-up scrubbed off. Even late night in a petrol station kiosk someone will spot a trace of eyeliner. Did all that really happen? One minute the street; next minute... Going out to these parties can get addictive; it can take over. Best to leave town if you are serious about work or study; and then come back on your own terms as a tourist to party.

I had always been officially 'underweight' with a twenty-eight inch waist (the BMI needs ripping up) but climbing had given me a toned body, still retaining skinny wrists and ankles and a slender form. I do not have much body hair, not much of an Adam's apple, I have a slim neck with square shoulders, no traps or bulging biceps and at that time my beard was light. I was shaving my legs. (Tanning is also essential). Holly Woodlawn, one of Andy Warhol's queens, once reputedly said, "I shaved my legs and then I became a girl". People were coming over to me in the clubs and telling me that I had a fabulous body and amazing legs. I realised that I dragged up well. The look was improving bit by bit. I was developing a girlie, slightly exaggerated OTT look. Here was something where I stood out and the feedback was good. I was veering more towards 'drag queen' than tranny though I have always been a bit fluid on that. I bought a sewing machine and was raiding remnant bins in Berwick Street. The staff at Borowicks were used to me (and all the other queens and wannabees in town) buying yards of spangly lycra and fishing the bins for cheap scraps.

Finally, I made it to the Wayout Club. This is the most famous, long-established tranny club in London – (of course, there is also Ted's Place before you snap at me). Wayout is a legend. The cellar bars it inhabits (always those steps, the first test in using heels) in the Tower Hill area has been presided over by Vicky Lee and partner Steffan Whitfield for a long, long time. (Steffan passed away in 2005 and was a celebrity T-girl). Every T-girl goes there at some point and anyone can pop up (I spotted a college Librarian one night in admirer mode). The black cabs waiting outside in a row at the end of the night are a familiar sight too, wonder why.... I went a number of times to the club when it was in Minories, Tower Hill (it seems to be back there now). Vicky Lee and Steffan were always very friendly. Wayout was in the same league of fame as Ron Storme's (which ceased in 2000).

Ron Storme was a prolific drag queen, It-girl around town and event organiser (probably one of the first) who started up many tranny events, many, many decades before I turned up on his doorstep. He was a legend and an instigator. It is rumoured that the Krays supported one of his 'drag balls' which were held at the Porchester. Ron Storme died shortly after I was getting to know the scene.

His latest venue in my time was in the East End of London, billed the 'Club Travestie Extraordinaire', in Stepney, of all places. It was once a month, I think... or was it? You always had to know about the 'second Tuesday' or 'third Friday' or suchlike, when the event ran. It became hugely famous and an established fixture. A doorman in bow-tie and dinner jacket (reputed to be Ron himself before he put the slap on) would ask everyone "do you know what night it is?" Then he would let you in. Ron Storme's and the Wayout were not sex clubs. You went there to socialise, dress up and have a whacky time of it.

There were other tranny clubs in the East End. It seemed at one point a hub of clubs which was strange considering it has an aura of being a very straight, non-gender-fluid, hetero-type of place – or maybe not! I once went to a pub called 'The Birdcage' (not the famous one). It was surrounded by a large housing estate – there were only the two of us in the bar which was billed as T-friendly. I was nervous, but nothing happened. It was all an adventure; trannying about town. Many trannies have got guts of steel; they do not give a shit and will go anywhere. We once got stuck on the tube: I was with Ritzy Crackers, drag queen. We lost our tickets for starters. We were wearing my baby pink and bright blue fur coats (shaggy pile, high-cropped with big white buttons – which I had made). We ended up going to a manager's office and asking for free tickets. You feel very vulnerable but it is only clothing. The only difference between a pair of cycling shorts and a mini skirt is a couple of seams; but those unstitched seams can get you into a lot of bother, strangely.

I was meeting lots of other people, making a big circle of contacts, making friends; all queens and trannies. In London there are a lot of fake people. They give you a card only to show off. They have no intention of doing anything for you. There were exceptions.

One night, artist, Sara Davidmann, turned up at the Wayout Club taking photos. At that point Sara only had a basic point-and-shoot camera and was more artist than photographer. This was the start of an epic journey for her. She photographed me and we made contact afterwards. I became one of her photographic muses for a while and we became good friends. I really did like her. Sara was going round all of the clubs snapping all the queens, CDs and transsexuals in town. Sara then pulled a masterstroke. With a friend of hers, Les, happy to help out with the driving, she hired a mini-bus and persuaded half a dozen London queens and trannies, her photo subjects: including Ruby Venezuala, other notables – and myself – to attend the opening of her exhibition of photographs, *Orlando's Butterflies*, at the Museum of Modern Art, Oxford, (downstairs galleries), in 2000). We were to dress up, of course. I will always remember, Ruby, in full-

Monty cabaret-drag, on the way back to town, stopping the car and pissing in a plant pot outside a hotel.

I underwent hours of photo shoots with Sara in her new studio. She was almost going blind trying to focus her new medium format film camera, with a manual focus screen (where the two ellipsis had to align). She liked me looking part-masculine, part femme and variations on all. We did a few naughty shots, quite provocative (nothing extreme like Mapplethorpe's fisting shot). Sara was certainly no prude having previously, for a project, taken plaster casts of cocks, turned them out in clay, decorated them and exhibited them (the casts!)

Sara became fascinated with the trans world. Her small hard-back book which followed featured many of us with photos and interviews. I believe it is still a major contribution to the history and records of the trans community. It was very nicely produced. It is of its time and some of those featured may not be with us now. I knew most of the girls and queens in it. By the time the book came out, I was working in clubs and had changed my look a fair bit, so they were not the most flattering shots of me – as I thought – but they were not faked up glamour shots. It is still a remarkable work. At least the subjects can speak for themselves in it.

The Wayout club is, like any club, hit and miss. You have to go and not expect anything. It is usually a rip-rollocking, zany affair and if it is your first visit to a T-club your head will still be spinning a week later. The drag show is usually a temporary annoyance, but mixes the night up a bit and you can stand and eyeball people while it is on – then dutifully clap and return to posing and catching admirers' glances. You do find that once admirers have bought you a drink they think they have paid for it. You need to be straight with them if you are not interested. A minute later they will have moved on to another girl. Getting chatted up is a badge of office and shows off to the others. Do not be nasty to admirers. They are putting themselves out too.

Ps: The Wayout Club has, again, moved venue. I do not like the look of the new place or the area; time will tell and I have not visited; watch this space.

Chapter 4
Soho, Heaven and
Transformer's Bedsit

The most famous gay nightclub in the world is under the arches in Charing Cross (they are always under some arches). The first time I ever went there, I queued up for an hour to get in. The queues went all down the street and round the corner.

> There was excitement in the queue. Behind me, as I turned into his conversation, a veteran of the scene reminisces on former visits.
>
> I knew I was entering a great place, a place with history, a place with a vibe, a place for us. It had had its fair ups and downs, the usual invasion of straights, bad reviews and more, but then, even though the great days were over (they always are) it still enjoyed, in the late nineties/early 2000s a sparkling time again. The club itself was nothing to speak of architecturally. It was a typical rough sort of night-club interior: low lighting, stone walls, sticky floors, with various bars dotted about and a few levels with different rooms pumping out ear-splitting beats. It was, as usual, the people who made it what it was.

I met Rex, at Heaven nightclub. He was fresh off the train from Peterborough, of all places. We were both queens on the make and we trotted around town together for a few days. He was staying at a hostel at Centre Point and doing okay getting free stuff. We became friends, no more. He eventually lived a few blocks from Stunners Club in Cable Street. (Stunners closed years ago; it was a legend). Once, after a walk-about town Rex threatened to burn his white PVC thigh boots as they pinched his toes so much. In the sanctuary of the Old Compton Café, she said to me, "only size eight feet", "you lucky bitch, I wish I could shrink my xxxxing feet – and you have got no Adam's apple". Here was a world where I had some advantages. Rex, (a.k.a. Candy Bar and later on, Ritzy Crackers) was a very creative drag queen and ended up a leading light on the club scene in town.

We would meet at the Old Compton Café (now Ballans) in the early evening and had the cheek to do our make-up at the tables. Then we would pop outfits on in the café's bogs or at Heaven nightclub. Once the barista in the café told me off for stinking the place out with my nail varnish; but they were fairly tolerant with us. The café was an amazing place. It went on for twenty-four hours. After the clubs finished, everyone (and all the drag queens) ended up there. You would sit there with a coffee for hours and chat to different people as they came and went – all night. It was the equivalent of the late eighteenth century coffee shop – Boswell's 'cheap club'. At about three am, they shut the place for an hour to swab the floors down and then it re-opened. The burly doorman had seen it all before.

> Into the night, a customer exudes a loud, long, shrill, camp, slightly lisping screech in conversation with friends. The doorman bounces over and shouts, "hey, you, why you mak-a' dat noise?" Neat looking camp guy with a shrug: "becothz...(with perfect lisp)...becosthz....I am a homo...thexshual..."

The café was a big part of the scene in Soho. We avoided any venue that looked vaguely straight. I never really explored the other bars and venues in the street.

Soho became a mecca for us. It was the only place in town we felt vaguely safe. It also had fabric and record shops and you would always bump into someone you knew there. Soho had another whole side that we barely knew of. The *FACE* magazine once had their office there, up a flight of stairs in a dingy room; which Neville Brody said (in his book), always shocked people, probably expecting Trump Plaza. Many media companies and creatives worked there cheek by jowl with the scruffy adult shops – and one or two supposed brothels (one place on the corner still had signs with *'Girlz, Girlz, Girlz'* outside) but everyone always said, "there never was any actual sex in Soho".

Soho had always been a bit rough round the edges: drug dealers, sex-shops, peep-shows, titty-bars and noise from all the glass collections at three in the morning. But if you want a quiet life, go and live in Kings' Langley.

Peep shows! Yes, they existed. I went to (probably) the last one or two that existed in Soho, on a school break in the 1980s. You stood in a cubicle, put 50p in a slot and a letter box flipped up and some bored looking girl gyrated about in soft, yellowish lighting. These were all run or managed by disgusting, greasy, nasty types. You knew they were still in town twenty years on, lurking about down steps and alleyways.

'V' (drag king) and I were dressed up, having high-jinks in the west end and coming back into Soho, we passed by the down-steps to one of these titty-bar-con-shops. The front-guy called up "come on down, the boss wants to meet you". Of course, when we got down and inside, they wanted to have a laugh at us. We exited quickly and I was very close to returning after dark with a big bucket of black gloss to decorate the steps. I could not believe these flea pit-con-shops still existed, right next to chic coffee shops, gay bars and bookshops. But that's Soho for you, rough around the edges – they have probably cleared out all the refuse and the good stuff by now as the corporations and the council want to sanitise it all and re-create Bohemia in their own image. Soho is now (and I have not been there for ages) struggling with the council who want to shish it all up, get rid of the Bohemia and edgy night-life that people came for in the first place and re-invent it as a posh shopping arcade. If a new Bohemia or gay mecca could emerge somewhere else; then in time, it too will be crushed by the improvers, the authorities and invaders. (See appendix 1)

When we were in Soho, we all walked down Old Compton Street, as if *we* owned it – it was the safest place we knew. I once saw Evita, drag queen at Heaven, six-foot at least, skinny as me, striding down the road with nine inch heels, not a wobble. I saw Peter O'Toole walking into the street, looking fabulous in a trench coat on another occasion.   One early evening, we were turning into Old Compton Street, on foot, dressed up, when a smart, white cabriolet cruised by in the traffic flow and a guy (with a lady seated next to him), shouted out at us, "SODOMITES!" He had obviously decided to turn into the street to shout some abuse at someone.

I was shouted at and called a "whore" wearing white stiletto thigh boots: quite a compliment actually. There were those ultra-cheap Italian restaurants selling bowls of pasta and the convenience store that looked like a time-warp. I remember a certain dandy who would sometimes pop into the Old Compton café: neat, clipped tache and with a gold-topped walking cane, he looked exactly like Sammy Davies Jr. My drag king friend quipped, "bet he hasn't worked for years". These were the people who were out of normal, vanilla society and did their own thing; at least until they hit thirty and then they started working in the finance department at John Lewis (as a queen friend did).

After make-up in the café, Candy Bar and I would walk down the Charing Cross Road to Heaven. Heaven club on a Wednesday was *the* religious service of the week for us. On-route, we would get the friendly "Oy, geezer bird" from some. Others were different. It was vitriolic hatred. "Yo, batty-boi", "where you go batty boi", "wha'ya do, batty-boi", "yo, is it dat you take dat …. up ya' batty?!" We had a few major incidents, but luckily we never were hurt. Others have not been so lucky.

Young gays come to London thinking it will all be so fabulous; they will have total freedom and acceptance of who they are – and they are so wrong. Recently a young, gay, YouTuber from small town America was in the news saying "I wore a flowery shirt in London and was verbally abused!" I wish I could have advised him before he came to London that it is full of homophobes and sulky gits. When I think of the chances we took then… it is probably worse now; probably get knifed in seconds.

Early days at Heaven nightclub involved changing in the bogs in the club unless we had used the cafe in Soho – or even a doorway or the end of Villiers Street (yes, it happened). One night, after getting in, someone standing by a bar downstairs; he had been on the door doing the guest list, said to me, "you should have walked straight up to the door, if you are dressed". It may not sound like much, but to us, it was a miracle to walk straight past the mile-long queue with your best mincing walk and straight in the door.

'Transformer' guarded the door on Wednesday evening. This non-gender specific, super-being appeared about ten feet tall with twelve inch plus polystyrene platforms and a one metre high headdress. Transformer's creations were on a large scale. I thought that this combination of monumental headdress and glittered-up-kitsch must have needed a mini-bus to get about with. I later saw that it was all packed down cleverly. He would turn up with a large plastic bucket and out came all the bits and usually the bucket or bin was part of the outfit of the trunk part.

Burnel Penhaul, a.k.a Transformer had been to all the great clubs, the legends; he knew everyone, he worked in clubs in London and nationally and he had won Alternative Miss World in 1991.†

We did (literally) look up to him. He was educated with a science degree. He came to London in 1989. He was trained in stage management. (LGBT archive.uk). Somehow, like us, he drifted into the addictive, time-consuming and exhibitionist world of the London dress-up scene, instead of getting a haircut and a proper job.

He achieved some lasting fame, standing for election in the Tatton constituency in the 1997 general election; the famous 'anti-sleeze seat. How Burnel got to stand I do not know. Perhaps, as he represented 'Miss Moneypenny's Glamorous One Party', Moneypenny's nightclubs had put him up to it, or paid his deposit. He lost the deposit, but getting one-hundred-and-twenty-eight votes, he beat the two other independents and all the 'others'. David Dimbleby rather spoils the moment with his clean cut, straight-laced commentary as the votes were announced. The major contenders all looked nervous. There was a lot at stake here and Burnel (Miss Moneypenny) looked ravishing with a monster headdress and had picked a good seat for a PR stunt. Maybe Burnel was anti-sleaze for real. Dimbleby warmly mentions the 'transvestite' in the group behind the returning officer – best of British luck and why not – is what he did not say but I know that he was thinking. Burnel, presumably would have been horrified by his 'transvestite' classification – but why should DB know the difference between a living art-work-costume-artiste and a tranny? It does beg the question, what Burnel would have worn in the Commons? Well, if women can wear make-up, outrageous hair colours and pink jackets in Westminster...

Transformer would let us through the door at Heaven with some friendly, facetious comments in the vein of... "Miss Thaang... I will be checking the stitching on your new outfit later on" – in his trademark, croaky, feminine, tobacco-grizzled voice; presumably based on an ageing 1950s American heiress or a penniless, former It-girl. It was all about gross pastiche.

He *was* the door at Heaven. This *was* 'Fruit Machine' on a Wednesday night – the night all the queens came to Heaven. He would put us on the guest list if we rang him in the week. He had been given a chance to take over Heaven's drab little coffee shop (a smaller archway) somewhere at the back of the club (the whole club was a series of under-railway arches). Every Wednesday, he transformed it from scratch into a camp paradise. He decorated the wooden seating with fabrics, coverings and kitsch props; there was a small fountain and he even bought food in for all the starving queens.

The 'Bedsit' as it was billed (in OTT imitation of all the bedsits we all lived in) became the campest, whackiest, most Bohemian legend of them all. People came from far and wide. Transformer, set it up every week, helped by a friend, Mick, who loved it all and was always there looking at us 'freaks' with wonderment. (Burnel once dressed up Mick in one of his outfits which was hilarious and it was like seeing in double vision; he would do this occasionally to chosen people, as in a music video he appeared in). Paul Neesham (a creative dress-up, artist and musician) also joined in supporting the night with spectacular make-up and outfits. Paul used to do zany looks: his head sometimes all white with bumps and odd deformities, all covered in thick make-up, with lips offset or completely around the side of his face and a bulbous end to his nose. My favourite was his 'ice-cream' head with a cornet hat.

We 'freaks' became part of the Bedsit and our lives revolved around it for two years.

Somehow, one night, I managed to get in the front door of Heaven before the club officially opened and get changed 'back-of-shop' with Transformer in the commodious staff bogs – which was a major coup. This was better than using the café or the club's bogs. In no time, I was joined by one or two others I let in on the secret – and before long there was quite a posse of us attached to and very loyal to the Bedsit and all getting changed in comfort before the club opened. Transformer did not quite know what to make of us. He kept saying we were not his girls, but we thought that we were. We were the 'dress-ups' and the 'freaks' mentioned on the Heaven website. We competed with Miss Kimberly's 'Powder Room' upstairs. She had a posse of regular drag queens hosting the upstairs bar and stage area and Miss Kimberly was the officially named host of the night.

I met some fabulous people in the Bedsit and made long-term friends. Miss Thierry was one of them. An ultra-creative, artistic-dress-up: young, French and new to London, His English was very good. He was far from home and pursuing the dream where the London streets were supposed to be coloured pink and studded with gold coins and rainbow flowers. His outfits and looks were amazing – more Priscilla than tart-whore like me. We became best friends.

After dressing up at a party somewhere, Miss Thierry, obviously networking well, earned a job as a 'duty manager' at the exclusive Home House private members' club in Portman Square. This was a very fancy place (originally an aristocrat's London pad) and now a top A-list hangout. Thierry, (as male) was on surprisingly good money now and he rented a flat in Great Windmill Street. The tiny flat was up five flights of stairs: a titty-bar was right underneath with its front kiosk almost touching the pavement and the 'Windmill' strip club was on the corner.

We hung out in the flat, made toasties and 'did the town'. A little posse of us developed around the flat and many interesting characters dropped in and out. A pastry chef, Lola, who worked in private houses, cheffing, joined us. He and I went on a mad caper around London carrying umbrellas and wearing bowler hats made by Lock & Co. from my dad's bits. When you are young you do spur of the moment things that make you sweat a bit thinking about them in later life, "did we really do that!?"

We had some fabulous parties at Great Windmill Street, hosted by Miss Thierry. They were wild — and friends and queens turned up dressed. Some of the local Chinese community were also in and out, leaving loaves of sweet bread and other strange culinary oddities. Somehow, Thierry would find all these people and characters. They were all great and there was a big vibe around the tiny flat.

I would pop into Home House occasionally. Robin Dutt, the London dandy (and journalist/writer), would be there, wafting about in embroidered frock coat. (I heard that he used to dress up on the tube and had nerves of steel). I remember once passing Tim Roth, actor, on the stairs; that was the sort of place it was, wall to wall with celebrities. Miss Thierry showed me the suite that Madonna was ensconced in while her London house was being decorated - and we sat in the bath.

Every Wednesday night at Heaven was madness. Transformer usually arranged a small show. One night, Candy-Bar and I were 'married'. The room was packed out and Boy George turned up, edging his way through to take a look. He was a good friend of Transformers and had probably caved in after nagging to finally show up and see what all the fuss was about. The next week Candy-Bar gave birth – to a doll, which was whipped out from under the bench seating and an umbilical cord was cut (possibly an echo of a

Leigh Bowery act there). Transformer had a collection of these dolls for outfit use. One outfit of his consisted of a headdress with coke-bottles (as test-tubes) containing foetus like dolls. He was extreme. His clock outfit and the birdcage were memorable to many. He would invite celebrity artists to perform. A male singer arrived one night (I did not know who) and Transformer stood in great reverential silence and stasis for fifteen minutes – a rarity for him – while listening to the piece. Miss Thierry and I did a small show as part of a competition. Miss Thierry wore a Transformer-faced-mask and black outfit and sported a strap-on, big, black rubber dildo which I started sucking, then I tipped yoghurt all over it. I have a rare photo of this masterpiece of entertainment and a seated couple have an astonished look on their faces. Transformer gave us first prize.

Transformer liked agitating people. If it was quiet in the Bedsit, he would move around the tables sticking his stripey-stockinged arse in people's faces, shifting the tempo up a bit. He DJ'd classics, like *Yes Sir, I Can Boogie.* If I hear them now, I am right back there. Transformer could be brutal. We were once all getting made up round a mirror. Someone was talking about a possible drag job or opportunity. Transformer quipped, "honey... it ain't ever goin'na happen" in his quasi-American crackling, ageing It-girl voice. He was right, of course. Some did make it. Bits of adverts, bits of telly...*everyone in Hollywood wants to be a star...*

It was a few years of having fun and expressing yourself; and it had to be more interesting than many people's lives. We were hard-up unless one was a trustafarian – or had a proper job. Some took to living in squats and eventually, most had to leave London when they ran out of money and had to go back to their provincial shit-holes and make do with one gay night, once a month in a straight club. More parallels with young Boswell's final realisation that it was not going to happen in London and that many Londoners were all 'fake' and looking out for number one.

More Bedsit: The egg and spoon race, where my Terry de Havilland six inch white platforms with buckled straps (bought from 'Cobblers to the World', The Stables, Camden Market, a famous niche shop – which was staffed by a corset wearing, black-haired goddess) – the heel snapped off. Transformer said they were shite-quality; The photo shoot for the club flyers. I did not know it was on and turned up that night in my most boring outfit – Miss Thierry never stopped taking the piss for that; The straight couple fucking on the floor one night; The time I ate fag-buts from an ashtray – I thought they were peanuts as my eyes were not lasered yet. Miss Thierry never stopped reminding me of that one. It is incredible that smoking was allowed in clubs. All our outfits had fag-burn-holes in them from pissed-up clubbers who would brush you on the dance floors, burning you with their ciggies and depositing a patch of fresh sweat on your arm as an added extra as they stumbled past, eyeballs like saucers. We did not stray far from our haven, with occasional forays out to other strange parts of the club and the cavernous main dance floor with the big-ticket shows.

At about three in the morning, when all the make-up was cracking, lipstick smudged and the food around the fountain was gobbled, Transformer would announce in his croaky voice, "coaches and carriages... coaches and carriages everyone". It was then all over for another week, which was the saddest part of the week for us.

Eventually, we were given drinks tickets, about three per night (Transformer handed them out to us like sweeties to his children). By now there was quite a little community of us. Everyone's look was evolving and improving and we were busy making new outfits each week. An Italian queen, Fabio, joined us and when another new young aspiring queen turned up, after make-up and outfits were on – she turned round and said, "Xxxx me Tracy, you've got better legs than me".

This was better than having sand kicked in your face and having to buy the Charles Atlas course (Marvel Comic adverts: "Skinny men, don't get sand kicked in your face!"...). Different worlds = Different values. In gay clubland, we had some value. We would scan the gay press each week to see if our photos were in the 'party' shots compilations.

The only problem was that everyone preferred you in your drag-character. As yourself, you were sniffed at or met with alarming stares or scrunched lips. This was a total reversal from the 'real world' of horrors; but then the alternative world can become more real than the real world. Your acquired persona takes over, as actors use their stage names and get typecast.

Many state that femininity (as we generally understand that term) is a mask: comprising an act and it can be acquired, studied and cultivated; are aspects of it congenital?

In a Poirot episode the other night, Capt. Hastings was amazed (and depressed) by a female character's transformation from a dazzling glamour puss to dowdy frump. It is all smoke and mirrors.

When out and dressed up, you take delight in not having to cover up any minor natural feminine traits or gestures that you normally have to hide in male-mode. In fact it is expected that you exaggerate anything feminine and to do 'man stuff' is a big *faux pas* – as is revealing yourself in man-mode unless you are with very close friends. It is best to let the illusion remain.

Burnel died in 2002. The Bedsit ended. I remember at the time when he was in hospital, we were all very sad and his death was a shock to our community. Some still keep up an internet presence of his highlights and Thierry talked about him and the Bedsit in a documentary about club life and dressing up in 2010. I do not think Heaven Club have done anything with that level of initiative since; preferring mainstream and bland like most big clubs.

I notice that internet mentions of the Bedsit and images of it are now getting sparser. One Alex Gerry, has published a large collection on-line. More content for the National Museum of Drag?

Here are some memories from Jessica.

"I was a teenager and had just run away to London. They would not let me in to Heaven nightclub as I was under age. So my friend, PJay, dressed me up and put me 'in drag' - as he said that I was very effeminate. As we waited in the queue there was this fantastic piece of art walking up and down the queue: the insatiable 'Transformer' (a.k.a. Burnel Penhaul). She came over to me and said "Why hello there Miss Thiang! Come in to the club" and then she walked me in. Transformer's outfits where so creative; she was literally a transformer. One day she would be dressed as Big Ben and another day as a big heart with arrows through it, with the most amazing headdresses and shoes made of polystyrene around 15 inches tall. I was in awe of her and every Wednesday night, I would be excited to see what creation or masterpiece she would have created to dress herself in. She offered me a job for £25 a night and some drinks' tickets which was amazing considering I wasn't even meant to be in the venue. And as I looked like 'Cher on smack' my name was Miss Trish.

There was Transformer, Polly, Miss Thierry, Ritzy Crackers and Tracy Tramp; who all worked in the Bedsit and they were just some of the cast working there. There was a dress up box in the corner and we all dressed up outrageously and camped it up while doing shows and having a ball. It was also at Fruit Machine (the name of the night when the Bedsit was on) that I met one of my best friends - and I still know her well; one of the hosts, Miss Glendora Mucklefanny. Eventually, Paul Churchill and David Inches (general managers at Heaven) realised that I was under age (after about three months) and I was told to come back when I was eighteen.

I went on to become a bit of a scene entity in my own right, known as 'Barbara Bush' and I then went on to transition and metamorphosis into the lady that I have become today, Jessica James. I am forever grateful to Burnel for offering me my first paid gig in London. He gave me so much advice and he was just a very special human being. He even called my dad "Miss Thiang" when he met him; that made my dad really laugh and smile. Thanks to Burnel, I felt welcomed into the gay scene and this helped me to know, in the early days, that this was the path I wanted to pursue on the gay scene. This helped me in deciding to become a singer and performance artist instead of a chef. This changed my direction in life entirely and for the better!

I send a 'big love' to Burnel who deserves remembrance and adoration".

Jessica James.

While living with my fetish club scene friends (they were very hospitable), with my sewing machine set up in the kitchen, I made (or engineered) a bikini-bra-top ensemble. I experimented with various combos of spaghetti strapping that would hold everything in place – it was a knotting challenge to step into it, straps in, legs through...but it worked and I have never seen anyone do this before or after; though I have seen fabric strips wrapped around the body which is tricky to get right.

The glowing lycra colours popped out in club lighting. A fake tan and smooth skin complimented it well. The strappy suits (optimistically noted as suits they only covered about 5% of my flesh) were sometimes finished with a cock-ring at the back holding various straps in union. It used to be muted that fashion designers would go round the clubs to be inspired by the creations of 'club kids' and sometimes I was sure that some fashion item in the shops was similar to something one of us had made or worn in a particular way months ago...Thierry sprayed bleach on his jeans long before ripped and bleached splattered jeans were sold in Top Shop.

I needed to push the look a bit further, so I made a cartwheel hat in Audrey Hepburn style. Mine was about one metre wide. It was structured with armature wire and covered with silky, dark blue, large polka-dot fabric, with a white lining under the brim and a big, white, silky bow. I carried it on the tube in a bin-liner. The hat was a hit and immediately said 'drag'. I also made some bright fake-fur, cropped coats: pink, baby blue and white.

The hat attracted *some* attention. One busy night in the Bedsit, a very camp guy marched up to me and said, "ya hat's TOOO BIG".

Sometime later, we were often in Brighton as Miss Thierry had made friends there. Miss Thierry knew Dolf and Brad who were T-shirt moguls and lived in a huge, posh seafront flat. Thierry would stay with them. At this later time, I was living not far off too. (Miss) Thierry and I were lured to a dressy, 'garden party' by a Brightonian friend, Neil. Drag queens were expected. Neil was a lovely guy and a very talented dressmaker, tailor and costumier. He could run up a man's suit (for party-wear) in shiny purple, in a day, to wear just for a night. We all trouped off to this posh party held in a big half-timbered pad somewhere near Brighton. I felt like a bit of a dick actually as it was broad daylight – anyway we were too far into this to back out now. The usual promises of "oh, you could meet interesting people and you will get a free feed.." It was fairly deathly as these parties usually are. The two hosts were pleasant enough. They were antique dealers apparently. Naturally, I wore the hat. After a while wandering around, I found a few trannies (birds of a feather) and I was talking to a couple of them by the garden wall. Then I heard some camp, shrill sounds and a queeny sort of guy marched up right behind me, saying loudly, "I luuurve the hat"; I had half turned, but was suspicious as the tone was not quite right. He walked straight past me not looking at me – and right up to the tranny I was talking to, who was wearing the most insignificant hat you can imagine – something like a black fez with a piece of netting stuck to it. I think I had outdone a woman's hat – worn by camp guy's friend – they probably went shopping for it together.

† The first daytime Alternative Miss World, 1991, was won by the "evermore infamous" Burnel Penhaul (Transformer) as Miss Galeforce Wind.
Burnel Penhaul also designed the costume for Molly Ratcliffe, who entered and won the 1995 Alternative Miss World as 'Mademoiselle Jean D'Arc'.

Alternative Miss World, created by Andrew Logan, artist and sculptor, is held every few years, since 1972. Andrew Logan made a sculpture of Burnel (of his head and ruff) which is very lifelike.
Looking through the back catalogue of photos over the years, you can see that Burnel was inspired by and part of this dress-up set. You can sense a particular style running through the events or more a way of thinking; as apart from other dress-up scenes.

https://alternativemissworld.co.uk/galleries/
Thanks to Andrew Logan's office for information and see:
www.alternativemissworld.co.uk

Chapter 5
Clubland and adventures
1998-2001

I THOUGHT THAT I WAS LOOKING GOOD AT THIS STAGE; AT LEAST MY POPULARITY HELD THIS VISION OF MYSELF TRUE. I did not do all the shaping: pads, corsets and silicones. I kept a natural look. That was my statement. No surgery, oil implants or bits of polystyrene – in or out of the skin. The only thing you have to concede to is tucking a bit. Without that, you have a bulge at the front which looks ridiculous. I used to use small silicones (tits) put in specially stitched pockets in outfits, but I stopped doing that later on, to go totally natural; much better and less to worry about as those chicken breasts often slide out during sweaty club nights. I am not pretending to be a girl – just wearing what I want to wear. I was never like the archetypal drag queen, if such a thing exists, I was fairly unique.

I was becoming a well-known face on the London scene. With Thierry working at Home House (in stylish male mode – though his dressing up as Miss Thierry, was certainly no secret there), we were on every guest list in town and we always made an effort: free drinks everywhere and red-carpet treatment; red ropes deftly unclipped by big bouncers guarding swishy doors. The ultimate accolade though was to be 'working' – that is dressing up at a club or party and getting paid for it.

I have no idea why I picked the name Tracy. Once you pick a stage name you are stuck with it – and all your friends use that forever instead of your real name. I was Tracy Tramp. Transformer used to call me "Missss Tramp"; it amused him. My close friends called me 'skinny bitch'. If you see my pics you will see why. Tracy sounded fine; it used to be a man's name funnily enough. Some of the chickens at Heaven used to like to socialise with me in the Bedsit; maybe they thought I was an 'auntie' type. They had this marvellous intonation when starting a conversation with me: "Eyaahh...Trayce..."

Sometimes in normal life now, when I hear the name, I instinctively turn around, which can be a bit embarrassing.

It seems as that someone else has (intentionally or not) my name. I think the queen is from the U.S.A. so no hard feelings but I think she has hung up her heels now.

We were friendly with Alexi. He was a short, smart, Italian looking, young guy with a clipped goatee; he was some kind of manager at 'JoJos' in Soho (Madam JoJos, is no more). He was always there in the admission box at the front whenever I was there. JoJos was the famous drag-cabaret club in central Soho and popular with hen-nights. There was a campaign to save it and other historic venues in Soho but it is a lost battle now. Some of my friends worked at JoJos (as it was known). I once worked a night there for a hen party – lots of fun – I had no gear with me and they needed an extra urgently to serve drinks and I was on the spot, so I stripped down to a thong and served drinks to tables all night like that. One hen had her hand glued to my ass all night. I loved it.

Alexi told us that a certain West End club wanted a few of us on Saturday night for 'mix-and-mingle'. Probably the club had approached JoJos to find some drag queens – how else do you find drag queens if you are straight? Though I was not a JoJos queen, I was to be 'certainly included'.

L'Equipe Anglaise was a private members' club in Duke Street almost opposite Selfridge's café. It had been operated by Sharifi-Nia since 1982. It was an 'exclusive' members' club with 2,400 members. Prices were set high to keep the 'riff-raff' out. The frontage was unprepossessing but it was a refuge for celebrities, royalty and well-heeled singletons.

We were asked to turn up on a Saturday night. Desire: young, creative and Spanish, had amazing make-up and looked very cute. He worked at JoJos doing cabaret and was a bubble of eccentricity. With his friend 'Jay' and myself, we were the first there.

Photos of the rich and famous adorned the club's hallway with the odd framed shot of someone on a yacht. Celebs and A-listers (some cruelly said C-listers) could really relax at the club and be a bit naughty. L'Equipe was not a luxury venue like the Robert Adam designed Home House, with its gilded stairwells, polished furniture and chandeliers but it was a lot, lot nicer than Heaven – which was a bit of a dump really in the grand scheme of things. I always remember the glitter ball downstairs at L'Equipe. I often studied it. It had a solitary spotlight aimed at it; this magic ball of mirrors on a motor showered flecks of colour onto the walls and on to our shiny outfits. That was about the sum of the parts of the L'equipe lighting rig. Clubs are odd. Turn the lights on and they all look shocking.

'Sharifi' ran the club very well (according to his representations) at a City of Westminster, licensing sub-committee meeting, in 2002, for renewal of his licenses. The private club with 'dancing and dining facilities'; though not popular with a few local Marylebone residents, had few, if any, complaints properly substantiated; it operated very good door policies; and was a baby in comparison to many other nearby noisy venues. There were never more than about 350 guests in the club on a night and he had a license until six in the morning, which was needed as it was a late club. Apart from some paparazzi, there was not too much loitering or noise outside and his experienced doormen did not need to patrol the street. The elite clientele of about 700 active members, were not fazed by champagne prices of £2,400 a bottle or £300 a year membership. After 2004 his rent was going to rise considerably from £90,000 to £280,000 a year and that was probably to be the nail in the coffin, hammered again by developers who wanted the site for flats. The Marylebone residents were not giving any quarter to any operator in the vicinity; objecting as a matter of course to any venue operating past midnight. However, his license was renewed, complete with the 6am hours, Thursday-Sunday, with conditions that he kept the sound limiter set as discussed and members, those attending the private functions and specially booked taxis were encouraged to behave in a considerate manner outside the premises.

All these clubs are up, are down, are up and down again – with a new upstart every year creating a stir in the world of tittle-tattle; but L'Equipe had kept its flag flying for decades along with others of its class that only included "Annabels and the Tramp club", according to Sharifi.
I bet you are now thinking... if you met me at L'Equipe...

After a few Saturdays at L'Equipe, Alexi arranged for us to be paid which was good news. The work was 'mix-and-mingle': party, drink your free drinks, be outrageous and get paid for it. In no time, it became a regular Saturday night job. Sharifi wanted to recreate a sort of Studio 54; which was the ticket for us. We added outrageousness, colour, and entertained his wealthy members. The model agency above also supplied some more beautiful people who were always floating about on club nights. It was a mad, mad time. The club took a while to get going, but by two or three in the morning it could be manic. We had drinks tickets each night; they were worth quite a bit. Sharifi liked to cook. He would sometimes prepare a meal; a buffet in the hall at the back for private, pre-club parties. We were always welcome to any food and drink.

Sharifi could be a bit hot-tempered (not surprising considering his rents and the constant hassles of running a club), but he loved us. He did not say much to us, it was probably best that way. We never had a problem even if he was stomping about in a bad mood complaining about this or that or rationing toilet rolls out. A queen from JoJos, who was an extra one night, did get a little rap over the silicones for gobbling too many canapes, but we regulars all played the part and behaved well in that respect.

We enlarged our offering with Kitty Cartier (glam drag), Tamara (beautiful, girly), Miss Thierry (best friend) and many other talents like Joy who did fabulous man-drag. One memorable outfit of Joy's that I recall: blue spikey hair, blue-based make-up, blue-denim outfit decorated with studs and this whole piece of art gliding about on roller skates.

I became very good friends with Desire who was living with Jay south of the river. Jay's flat was very nice and we were often all round there. Jay had a good job but was once 'outed' (as a tranny) at work and after that he kept quieter about his after work shenanigans. He used to leave his flat dressed up, and drive into town. He was good looking, in a T-girl way, and his outfits became more creative in time. Above all things, Desire wanted to be a muscle-Mary, which I always thought was a shame as he dragged up well and was slim. They were both larger than life characters, not satisfied with a drab life or fitting in. I always mix best with counter-culture people or people who are not main stream. It is more difficult for them to criticise me when they are even odder!

We started working at the mid-week private parties at L'equipe. The first one we did exceeded everyone's expectations, Sharifi included, I am sure. We were asked to hover about the entrance as people came in and one of the first guests in was Prince Andrew (the party prince). He took it all in his stride; he walked past us at reception like any normal guest. Another guest to the same party was on the phone in the toilets soon after: "mum, you never guess who walked in..." This party was so A-list it was a bit staggering. I remember seeing Hugh Grant, Andrew Lloyd Webber, Lionel Ritchie and many more I did not recognise. We were then asked to do a wedding party (the bride was a club regular and a famous model). *Hello* magazine covered the event. They cruelly cut us out of the pics (even though the high profile couple themselves had asked for us to be there; though we had a laugh as Jay had managed to get his hand in one shot.

There followed a procession of parties for all sorts: corporates, banks (not the High Street type) and themed events. We became the new It-girls at the club and around town, ironically mimicking the real-life It-girls we would brush shoulders with. All kinds were in and out of the club: Naomi Campbell, Mick Jagger – and who knows who else I would not recognise in the half-dark with my short-sight. By this time we were dealing with the club directly; they paid us with cash on the nail each night; there was never any problem. Desire was funny. She would get bored near the end of the night and stomp about striking her hands together muttering, "I wanna' my money now".

Sharifi held a 'New York' party one night. There were hot-dog stands and popcorn carts dotted about and the whole club was turned into New York for one night only. We were all in position (at our own discretion) waiting for people to arrive, and Desire, who was mad, suddenly scooped hands into the popcorn bucket on the cart by her and threw a big handful of popcorn up in the air laughing like a child. At that exact moment, Sharifi walked by, crunching his feet through scattered popcorns. I thought, 'that's it, we're sacked'. Sharifi glanced sideways, chuckled and walked on. Then I knew what we were there for: Kitty Cartier dancing on the piano; myself crawling down a dinner table on my hands and knees wearing a pink bikini, getting my butt slapped; the buzz of the toilets, where all the action was; the people, the regulars; the strange nights where no-one turned up – or just a posse of bewildered looking girls from Abbot's Langley.

A member came in and walked up to me (from behind) I was at the end of the corridor near reception. Then he saw my face, drew back and smiled. Sharifi had warned him, but he thought I was real. Sharifi loved our shock value and I think he smiled a bit more when we were about.

We *were* the Jeffrey Hudsons – the dwarf who jumped out of a pie for Henrietta Maria (Scott's *Peveril of the Peak*). But who would have missed out on all that outrageous behaviour? We all thought we would make it. Many of us were signed to various useless London agencies, without much luck. This was 'us kids having fun' around town, as countless thousands have done before us – but there were not many of these jobs about. It must be worth a footnote in history. Okay half a footnote? Quarter? Come on..

> Exotic, creative characters at a dress-up party (or any situation they choose) are living artworks. They have spent hours, days or weeks getting their outfit or look together. What does an artist do creating a painting or sculpture that is so different? Artists usually show finished pieces in a gallery or location (rather than wearing them) to hushed murmurs of appreciation from bemused visitors who pretend they can read the bullshit mission statements accompanying each piece.
>
> As artists, dress-ups are questioning the imposed order. The creative-drag-club-kids are questioning conformity and order; perceived ideas on gender, dress and sexual stereotyping. They are doing exactly the same job as an 'artist' – asking us to question – and entertaining us. Some journalists and photographers have recorded some of the great club-nights in history, so we have some records.
>
> Partying or dressing up anywhere is very ephemeral like conceptual art. Beautiful pavement art washes away in a shower of rain. A pile of bricks is dismantled and set up again in another gallery. When the night finishes, the exotic characters all vanish – here one minute, then dismantled and gone to be re-created at another time and place.

A few well-heeled city-traders were regulars at the club and started promoting Saturday nights there. 'Gellofishpink' they called themselves. They were great guys. They loved us drag queens and they wanted us to stay on Saturdays. They hired a few DJs of their liking and put a banner up in the hallway and had some key-fobs made which I still have one. I have no idea why Sharifi bothered with it as the club seemed to run itself pretty much on its own. Sharifi went through a few 'promoters'.

I was usually early to work and straight down to the ladies' for make-up, well before people arrived at about 8 or 9pm – as there is nothing worse than being gawped at by anyone while transforming.

It is a convention that most trannies use the ladies. In some clubs no-one cares and the bogs are like an extension of the club and a free-flow for anyone. I always check first and if in a strange club go to the men's. It can be awkward in the men's. You are in no-man's land wherever you are. Unisex toilets are now quite common and this saves all the agro. I would rather have a broom cupboard to get some privacy.

Most of my fellow queens were changing at JoJos in Soho and arrived ready made-up and dressed at about ten. It is fun to make the grand entrance and have the rope lifted for you, but at 9 or 10pm there was no-one there to impress. I could not travel done up. Not worth the risk at all. Always see if there is changing and you can get in early. At some big events you have no choice and if you arrive in drab mode...you would be sent packing or to the back of the queue. There is a lot of logistics involved in getting to the door. I have changed in my car in a car park – quite common with T-girls. I have done exactly that in a car park ten metres from the Village a few times.

Once in the safety of the club bogs, in front of the cruel mirror, get organised. Make-up box open and things in order; foundation on quickly (unless you do contouring) and powder in well; then start the eyes. Once that big job is over, put the black liquids away, then do the blusher, lip-liner and fill in, gloss or shading. Maybe spray a fixer. Outfit on, accessories on, a squirt or two of Coco Chanel – and once the wig or hat is on, you are in character. Stumble up the stairs and dump bags in bag room. Make sure you have a small touch-up kit handy on you (lip-liner pencil, powder, lipstick and a small dab of foundation in a pot) in case you start falling apart later on (if it cracks up, you can sometimes smudge it all back together again). Re-do lips and you are good for another three hours. If you are lucky enough to have a locker, it is easier as you can do a proper re-touch job half-way through.

I am superstitious and often take: a spare wig; a spare outfit (in case anyone throws a drink over you – yes it happened, via a tranny in a fit of jealous rage) and spare shoes (shoes do tend to break and if so you can do nothing with them then). You can clip a couple of safety pins inside your handbag as these can repair clothing straps and splits or buttons and clasps on the spot. They also keep your car-keys and tickets safe. *No-one* will have a roll of gaffer tape behind the bar or a handy tube of Gorilla glue unless the maintenance man is at the party. Pack them in your main bag in the cloakroom – they could just... (in the words of the *Yellow Pages* ad)...save your life. When back at the hotel (if away on a jaunt) in the lack of a polystyrene head, take a large metal meat-hook. You can then hang the wig from the clothes rail or edge of the wardrobe to air it out and hang it straight. I also take a small 'hotel kit' with me including a small screwdriver set (great for removing window locks and then replacing them when you leave), pliers, sewing kit with tough black thread, small scissors and various safety pins. You could take some iron-on tape too. This is all for emergencies. If you always have all this, you will never need it. It takes up the space of a tiny wash bag

You can get the make-up time down with practice. Ruby Venezuala got it down to about ten minutes, it was amazing. By the time I was finished and up the stairs at the bag-room, the two (real) girls who were always behind the front desk were in place and the doormen were limbering up.

There were often private pre-parties before the main club doors opened at L'equipe. One night I walked into the back early and a Miss Internet Model competition was going on. Another night, a fancy dress party was in full flow pre 9pm. I mixed in oddly with the Princess Leias; a drag queen at a fancy dress party. A real one, or someone dressing up as a drag queen?

Footballers, bankers, models...more parties – and some very dull nights; an endless stream of unreality. The bouncers (ex-military and ex-police) were always friendly to us, we felt like we were safe – we were in a straight club, but we never had any trouble. The punters liked us. This was probably because they were more sophisticated and worldly than your average straight club-types. Celebrities are usually drag-queen friendly. Sometimes, it would get very exciting as the evening progressed. Real life It-girls, Lady Victoria Hervey or TP-T (Tara Palmer-Tomkinson) she was actually known by that acronym, would turn up; paparazzi would be outside the door. All of a sudden it was £200 to get in, 'for Champagne', of course.

We were now inside, looking out – what a change-up eh? People were asking *me* if I could get them on the guest list. I would sometimes wander to the front desk to look out and see what all the fuss was about outside. I liked the upstairs more. This was a big space at the back and it had a high ceiling; you could mince about in it properly – not so easy in the cosy, sometimes over-crowded and under-lit downstairs bar and dance floor, which we had to gravitate down to later on, as they closed the upstairs at about midnight.

One night, early on, before it was busy, a smart, well-mannered, preppy sort (worked in banking apparently or probably owned one) asked me downstairs to sit down and chat with him. He bought me a drink, which I always thought amusing when people did at the club as I had free drinks galore. He wanted to know what I was into. He wanted to experiment. I had to see what was going to happen here... I was whisked off to a Hotel in Earls Court near the Philbeach (I could only think of the Philbeach area, which was a T-girl centre at one point) so we ended up at one next door to that. It was a bit awkward really, as these things usually are. He felt a bit hot and bothered afterwards, but I told him he had nothing to worry about. This was all of my own volition, but it had to be done; where else could you do this? We were then back at the club and I was back to prancing about. I told Miss Thierry about it the next day and she thought it was all hilarious. I would never have let on who he was, even if I knew his name.

Dancing, parading about, exchanging sallies with customers and sipping our free drinks and eating canapés. It all ran smooth...week after week. A number of London queens would have cut their eyelashes off for our jobs.

By the early hours the downstairs bar at L'equipe was chock-a-block. The main barman was a suave hunk: square jaw and black shiny hair; and was like grease lightning with the bottles; Tom Cruise without the acrobatics. The bar was six deep at least. I enjoyed being in the bar throng: it was a good excuse to get close up to people (imagine all this before Coronavirus) and I had free drinks tickets anyway. Sometimes people would buy me a drink as well, much to my amusement.

When someone booked a party at the club they had to be confident that the bar would make £10,000 or something ridiculous like that. Often, the whole place rocked and felt like this was the 'it' place in town. I remember sitting on one of those padded seats downstairs with my leg draped over a model's shoulder, while she fed me Champagne from a bucket. TV cameras turned up one night; sometimes the place was like a morgue, with six people – but Sharifi did not seem to give a stuff. It was a member's club for well-heeled types and celebrities but sometimes more normal people seemed to turn up. There was never any trouble, not that I saw and there were no dodgy types hanging about outside either apart from some paparazzi; City of Westminster Council should have given Sharifi a medal; the council's business (supported by some residents) is to shut down all the West End nightlife, as apparently, some people want to sleep at night and also live in the party capital of Europe. Sell your London pad and get a ten-bed villa in the Highlands with 1000 acres, ten miles from a road.

I had a good repartee with the regular customers. I was having a conversation with one I had not seen before; he wanted to see me afterwards, changed as a guy. When the club was packing up, I came upstairs: now all washed off, puffa jacket on, woolly hat on, holding the suitcase with my gear (yes, all for a pink thong). I spotted the guy who was hanging about at reception. I went up to him and said, "Hi, it's me, remember, remember...the queen from before, Tracy..." His jaw hit the floor, he stood paralysed. Most of us do look very different once washed off and people cannot get rid of the image of you all done up.

On the night bus on the way out of town going down Oxford Street, a couple of young guys sitting next to me on the lower deck were talking about the club they had been to. They talked about 'so and so' dancing on the bar. I knew it was L'Equipe and Desire. They then said, "..and what about that one with the denim hot-pants, phhoarr". I would never spoil the illusion. Which is why, at a critical point in the night, it is time to go. Do not overstay and ruin the illusion with your tipsy self, looking like a sack-of-shit at three thirty in the morning. Always go while people remember how fabulous you were, as the zenith of the night crosses to last stragglers. Posh people know this technique very well. Lord Lieutenants never stay for the dance; just as the tables are being pulled aside, they doff their heads politely and say: "must get back...the dogs... you know.."

Time to go. 'Coaches and carriages', or a non-legit-taxi (they were cunning and did get under the club's radar sometimes), back to North London; a treat, which fairly ate up my money, but sometimes it was worth the comfort.

> The taxi driver pulls to a stop opposite my flat. I am just
> contemplating the dash across the Seven Sisters Road when he runs
> his hand down my leg and asks for some action – but I am too

blitzed by four in the morning. You only want to throw the shoes off, wash off, rub your eyes and relax – it sometimes seems a shame to take it all off. I remember occasional after-parties at someone's flat where some would only take the slap off in the early hours – even sleep in it – that is rough!

I do not know how it all eventually ended at the club. I think, like most things, it ran its course. I have subsequently found a mention to the effect: that we may *not* have been the first drag queens in this club – and that there was a prior attempt at what we were doing. No one at the club ever mentioned our predecessors and I am totally sure that nobody could have ever stepped into our stilettoes with as much style as us.

A noted promoter in town, Terry Smart, liked dress-ups and drag queens to be around when he was launching a new night. I was often hired. His aid-de-camp, once told me, "it's because you are the business, Tracy." We were at all sorts of glitzy clubs around town; some mainstream like Ministry of Sound (a massive, noisy, gaff) or the Café de Paris (finer but merely another club – which just recently announced its closure, very sad) – but dancing with the Marquess of Bath!

Sometimes we were asked to come and 'support' a new night, for a friend of a friend at a small boutique club tucked away somewhere. We would still make the effort and usually get free drinks and have a nice time. You certainly have a good time. Especially, if you are comfortable in your outfit and it is easy to wear.

Do not make the mistake of going 'casual' on a proper night out. Once, while trannying about town...

> We got into the hotel lift going down and a couple of other 'girls' jumped in. We were all heading to the bar round the corner. I was looking very glam, all pink and sparkling. One of our lift-sharers was in a denim jacket. I thought, 'No. For a big night out, look like a princess, not like you are going to the gym or out for coffee. I could feel that this girl was thinking "wish I had made more of an effort".

"Make-an-effort" was usually the sub-title to many dress-up parties. You can never really be overdressed anywhere unless you wear a dinner-suit and they are all in lounge suits (happened once in normal life) but who cares? Even Bridget Jones got it wrong. Being overdone is far better than being under-dressed which makes you cringe in a different way – and you spend all night apologizing and making excuses for your lack of effort. One trick is to hide in your car or in view of the entrance and observe people going in – then you can make quick adjustments. That can backfire if you missed seeing all the glam people who got there early or after you which is even worse. If you drive and park close, you can take a change of outfit in case. Follow your instincts on it, or get a whipping and go back a second time for victory. I once wore a big coat and kept it on for a bit. The partner comes in handy here, two of you the same and you can get away with anything.

I started up 'The Drag Queen Agency' and listed it for free in *Spotlight* (the main publication for anyone in the entertainment biz apart from *The Stage*). I had calls coming in. In fact from that free listing I was still getting calls from production companies, years after I had moved out of town. It could have been a winner. Before I left town, I tried handing it on to a queen friend but there was no interest. You have to be very careful of production companies. When they want something, they move heaven and earth. Then you can never find them when it's pay-time or you want photos from the show. If you merely sign on with agencies you will get nothing of any value unless you are a major talent, in which case you have a proper agent I assume. Film extra work is something all students do. You get very well fed and watered, though most of it is sitting about all day – then they cut everything. With drag jobs you need to be very, very careful to get paid on the nail too. Never, ever invoice, you will not get paid.

I was hired by the Royal Academy, (or promoters, I cannot remember which) to host at a glossy party in the summer of 2001 called Tango. I collected a few top queens together. No act was required. Juana la Cubana (an astounding drag queen of great experience) warned me about getting payment, but I said I would guarantee it to all the queens myself out of my own pocket. I wanted it to happen. This was quite some do. When we all got there, the others finally realised it was all for real and they were quite impressed. Imagine walking past Fergie, so close you can smell the toothpaste. She eschewed having her photo taken with us, as I later found out, reading Miss Kimberly's column in the gay press; also that there was an impressive roll call of famous WAGs there including

Ivana Trump. Not having my eyes lasered yet, I was virtually blind and hardly saw anyone, which is a good thing if you are nervous.

On arrival, wandering about the outer courtyard where all had gathered with drinks before going in, thankfully, there were a couple of familiar faces: the famous It-girl round town, (as opposed to my pastiche of one) Tara-Palmer-Tomkinson, who was very nice to me whenever we brushed bronzed shoulders in a club (she sadly died very young) and Nicky Haslam who had a photo column in *Hello* magazine and was quite a star in his own right, always very dapper and still looks fabulous.

You must understand that any queens are the hired entertainment; you do not know people there, but you rub shoulders with them – and it is a laugh – it has to be done; why not? However, as we 'mix-and-mingle', we have slightly more connection with the guests than the juggling act. It is *certain* that the one thing that everyone will remember afterwards and talk about is the drag queens; whether they liked them or not! The trouble started afterwards with the RA when I tried to get payment after 'no cash being available on the night'. It took some weeks and a few letters. Always make sure you get cash on the night if you are the clown.

Another queen and I had a spot on Richard and Judy – some background work. Richard and Judy were lovely people. Alexi organised it. He told me that we were getting paid and how much. You get treated very well on telly and film. There are nice dressing rooms and sometimes food and drink. It is a fun hour or two out, that's all. Enjoy it and do not analyse it too much. You have to sign release forms at every turn, very sensible for them; and I have asked models to do this on my own photo shoots, or they have you over a barrel. This was a fun day out but Alexi spoilt it all, when he refused to pay us afterwards! I was quite shocked as he gave no excuse and he had definitely said it was paid work and everything went very smoothly on the job. After I sent draft Sheriff Court papers to him (a good trick as there is no payment due just to get the forms, or it could be about £80+) he paid up.

I was photographed by Rankin once. A posse of queens were rounded up to his studio for a photo-shoot. Rankin had asked specifically for 'no make-up on at all' as he was doing some post editing to fit his brief. He would be 'arting up' our faces afterwards.

He also asked for us to wear black. I acquiesced perfectly to his instructions. Some did not and two others who turned up with full make-up on (very unprofessional for a shoot unless it's is only foundation) – they had to wash it all off! I did manage to get away with a touch of foundation though. It was a fun shoot – he was fascinated with some of my bawdy tales about multiple members and one hole. I have a test Polaroid from the shoot. He had said wear black, so I wore a black spaghetti-strap thong and matching top.

While the Bedsit was still going and Burnel was still with us, I was in Heaven late one Wednesday night, looking fairly drab in bell-bottomed jeans and my Terry de Havilland white, platform, block-heeled boots glued back together. Philip Sallon, 'the (other) party prince' was downstairs. He was a doyen of the club and a fashion and gay icon. He was wearing some kind of toga-type outfit and was being orbited by a couple of hangers-on. I was just about giving up the ghost and ready to leave as it was a bit flat by then, when Mr Sallon stopped me in my tracks and said, "Come to this party... here is the invite (it must have been the last one he had), it's a good one to go to... and you can bring a friend". He beautifully calligraphed my name, plus 'guest' on the card. I thanked him and he vanished into his orbit of admirers and the dark, smoky archways of the club.

I raced round to the back of the club to our home in the smaller archways and found Miss Thierry in the Bedsit and showed her the card; it was a big lavish card, with a sexy Aubrey Beardsley type illustration on the cover, with a huge member topping out in front. Miss T was impressed.

The theme was 'Dandy or Courtesan, strictly'.

Miss Thierry and I hatched plans and chose our outfits. One June evening in 2001 we made our way to a palazzo in Portland Place, for George O'Dowd's fortieth birthday party. We knew we were there as the freaks; we would not meet His Highness at any point – and it was going to be a laugh – expect no more. Free drinks and nibbles for skinny queens who never eat. As we entered, Nicky Haslam was there with a camera crew from *Hello* and they took our pic; he seemed pleased to see us. I had on a pink, PVC crop-top and mini, a white cropped, Chanel-cut fake-fur with oversized white buttons, various diamante pieces, blond hair and the hat. Miss Thierry had a huge beehive hair-do and a hooped, peach coloured dress on; very Marie Antoinette.

We entered the main room downstairs and Transformer was Dj-ing. Jonathan Ross and Venessa Feltz walked in the door a few minutes after that and threw up cameras at us. After the initial buzz of getting in, on closer inspection, most people seemed to be just wandering around and about: up and down the huge staircase, sliding hands down the polished hand-rail, peering through the bulbous, cast-iron balustrades and exploring this vast terraced town house. George and close pals must have been secreted away in special chambers. After a few tours of duty and when we thought everyone must have seen us at least twice, which is enough, we exeunted.

A few days later we were wandering about town looking for copies of *Hello* on the newsstands and spotted Philip Sallon doing the very same thing – still with the hangers-on in orbit and still in a toga (a different one, I presume, it must have been his toga-phase). I recently found out that he even lived in Dollis Hill, where I grew up. I probably passed him on the street in my youth). It was a fab spread in *Hello*. We had a centre-piece photo; I bet Mr O'Dowd was furious – 'who let those xxxxing drag queens in?'

Miss Thierry was mortified with her expression in our photo but I liked my pouty, haughty look. At last, *we* were the beautiful people (for one night only!) Quite a few personalities were on the page around us and at least we were actually named on the caption. Nicky Haslam had rung us to ask for our names. That was very nice of him; he was a drag fan.

Us 'freaks' were starting to be mentioned in the despatches of the tittle-tattle columnists.

If you can see it through properly, who knows where it could all lead...fame and fortune, a dozen sugar-daddies, a flat in the West End, house parties in the country...or sobbing into your wrinkled reflection from a cracked mirror in a lonely bedsit at the age of sixty-five; OK enough.

I did some very whacky jobs. In the days of the Bedsit, Transformer, was working for Miss Moneypenny's clubs. At one point he was the 'face of Moneypenny's'. Miss Moneypenny's is still going and they like to present as glamorous and a bit zany. To me they look like most club-nights for straight people, with the occasional drag-queen popping up, standing out like a sore thumb. Transformer got us a gig one night at a MP venue– that must have been the day I visited his flat in West Hampstead and saw his outfit collection; the whole place looked like a walk-in wardrobe – no idea what happened to them all – I think they were all destroyed. In the lack of a national drag museum it would have been difficult to house them anywhere. (There's an idea for any funda-holics).

It was fairly tedious at the club, the usual sort of thing; but we were paid. Later on I met a queen who travelled all over the UK doing Moneypenny's, which I assumed was some sort of club franchise as they were all over the place. We did a couple of them. We travelled by train all the way to the sticks and back. These were straight clubs with ordinary straight club kids. On one of these nights, I was part of a 'conga' line upstairs and a young lad came up behind me, clasped my waist, rubbing himself all over me – tart that I am, I let him do what he wanted. I must be convincing from the rear. When he saw my face – he went white and threw himself against a wall in disgust! What is the problem if you enjoyed it?

The scariest job I took, was the 'South Coast Weekender' (in 2000/2001). One Friday in April, I took the train from London to a holiday camp complex on the south coast (Pontins, I am sure). The promoters had contacted me, wanting a couple of queens to host the VIP room at their event. I went alone, unable to persuade anyone else to do it; which slightly disappointed me, as it was work. London queens will not go south of Brixton or north of Wembley Park. They are prima donnas and often complained about the slightest thing.

Come the evening, the VIP room was great and the usual M.O.; but outside that room as I wandered through one part of the club….I felt an empty coke can hit my head and a clubber growled some insult at me while he made an action with his leg as if he wanted to kick me to death. Back in the safety and civility of the VIP room a huge black guy, about six foot wide, looking exactly like a minder should look like, came over and said in a bass growl, "ere, the Boss wants to meet you". Not sure what he was the boss of, unless he meant the Guv'nor, or unless he was the actual promoter, I followed. Seated in a corner at the back of the room, wearing a glitzy jacket was the celebrity gangster, DC – he was also in the listings for an 'audience with' to promote his books and a film.

I gave him a twirl. He drawled, "yehh, wery nice". Then I was back to the bar chatting up the VIPs. I slept in one of the cabins in the camp, it was all quite bizarre – but I was treated well by my mysterious hirers.

Chapter 6
Kingly Street and Fitness First

I was living in a gay house share in a terraced street, Zealand Rd, which is just off the Roman Road. One tenant was Justin. Justin was the greatest person in the world, so I can mention him, I am sure he will not mind. My partner (who met him) always remembers his great tits – he was a regular muscle-Mary at clubs like Trade – he could do the tit-jiggle as they all did on the dance floor. He was an instructor at Fitness First, Kingly Street branch; (we used to call it Fatness Fast). Justin was then promoted to manager. Like all new leaders, he chose a few people he wanted to surround himself with and I started working there. Customer retention then sales and instructing (I was a climber so that was not so stupid).

Justin was a one off. The 'new member parties' were put on steroids, and since we were a spit from Soho (officially in it), he encouraged a few drag queen friends to turn up and for me to dress up; I was almost forced to. What a punishment. The parties went wild. Miss Thierry turned up and was joined by friend Dilza, a very cute Brazilian (real) girl who loved the scene and became very good friends with us both and we went around partying together; she was almost like family. Party pictures went up on the gym's walls and it was all sunshine. But there were mutterings and dissenters in the shadows and from behind the Smith machine. I got on very well with most of the instructors and staff (six of us shared a tiny cubicle office) but one or two...they would exit quickly before the parties and mutter and murmur. They did not like it one bit. It was too gay; even though plenty of real girls turned up and it was a great atmosphere.

The fitness instructor course, an entertaining diversion, was a first class torrent of wildness and excitement. It was a one week residential course for the Fitness First, YMCA instructor course in a FF gym out of London. It was a huge, spotless, place. The two course leaders never stopped reminding us they were ex-forces and were a bit straight-laced. It was a very thorough course. But it was more than lectures and instructors' exercises in the gym...

In the FF in-house magazine, they had published a shot of me from a party; back view, in a thong and wearing a military helmet and holding a plastic gun. Most knew about it. One bloke-type on the course, probably a queer basher in his spare time, was shown the pic. He reputedly said, "phhoarr, I'd give her one straight up there", thrusting his finger up my paper arse. He was fairly mortified when he was told, probably hung himself. In a lecture, the pic was produced and the girls were tittering over my thong...quick as a flash, I said: "well, my wife likes it". Discipline went right out of the window just then.

In the evenings we were in dorms and it was like being with students in halls of residence in the first week of term.

At the end of the course we had *the* party in the local bar. Always the final party just like a film. This was the highlight and I was going to dress up and shock one or two of them. Which happened when instructor, Ben, a muscular, straight-laced type who was worried if he thought his T-shirt looked too tight, turned round and then pretended to feel sick on sight of me. The chief cock-teaser in our group – a very pretty, luscious, gym-fit-type, she said to me, "as a man, hmm...but as a girl..." The week was a lot of fun and I know everyone still remembers everything.

I went to Desire's gym with him to give him a few tips as he was not getting anywhere. It was a huge, sterile, characterless, grey, chain gym: Holme's Place†, Oxford Street. I paid for a day pass. I was warming him up and trying to work out how he had injured his chest recently and suggesting a few gentle recovery exercises on the fit-ball, when a pettifogging instructor came over to us and said to me, "you can't wear that vest". "What?" "No, sorry, men are not allowed to wear sleeveless vests here – "but...." "yes, the women can". He shrugged and walked off. We walked out and I convinced Desire to join FF which he very much enjoyed.

Things carried on at the gym as usual but it was not long before Justin was busted. The mutterers and dissenters had their way. FF sent Justin to a branch in France (he was fluent in French) or so we were told. The new manager was a 'prick-eared Puritan'. I think he had 'cleaned up' other branches. He presented as a quiet non-aggressive type but he had a coat of thorns on underneath. The first thing he did was to take down all the party photos and then went on to remove any kind of fun or eccentricity about the place. I wish that the head honchos would not cave in to spoilers who make silly complaints. Here is a good example:

One instructor complained about our *Sales Bible,* named as such: a book which contained a written record of all the sales, in case the computer went kaput. His beef was, supposedly, with the title of this ledger on 'religious' grounds. So we renamed it *Sales Ledger* or something like that to placate the ignoramus. There were *no* philological grounds for this change at all. I will not go into it fully here, but I can tell you that to get rid of the word 'bible' was a ridiculous notion – bible being a word in common parlance in the English language to describe any 'authoritarian' work on a subject; and the word is Greek, not even Hebrew, nay not even Aramaic...nor would it have even have insulted a Babylonian to have used it.

After Justin's banishment, the branch ended up like all the others – corporate, bland and boring – and our posse dissipated. I went back there a few years ago and it is still there, down thirty steps and within a Teddy Boy's spit of Carnaby Street.

It now looks totally different inside: not such a friendly a feel to it, I think, and the drinks machine and seating at the front had gone (obviously to stop drag queens congregating). The instructor showing me around was friendly and I managed to glean that there still was some memory in the company of that wild period. It was a community back then and I made a lot of friends there.

†Known as Homos' place, with no justification!

Chapter 7
Fetish

EARLIER ON, AT A FETISH PARTY, I HAD MET a very nice guy called Jack. He had a partner Angie. They were a straight couple with very good jobs – they loved the fetish scene and went mad at weekends. They were very hospitable and generous. We started going to fetish parties together and a group of us developed as more waifs and strays were added to our clique. There was Dan, a young kid, fresh off the boat from Zimbabwe, a gay refugee; Ross, the actor (popped up in *The Bill* here and there and I am sure I have seen him in *Bridget Jones*); Mark, a stockbroker, trading 'ethical shares' and lots of others who popped up once in a while like TammyWhynot? from Seattle, USA, a public health official, who was always talking about hand-washing – this is over twenty years ago!

I was not into fetish really. I had started out by going to these parties as trannies were welcome and it was somewhere to go and flash your tits in public. Parties like 'Mass' at Brixton were huge and full of action. We went to them all. I went to 'Club Rub' by the Monument one night on my own. Rub was great, full of characters. I met a great pre-op girl. A lot of girls like other T-girls. We walked together through the night streets of the city, freezing cold and went back to my house share in Archway and we hung out for a few weeks.

Party night was *some* event. It started in Jack's nice flat in Docklands.

> We are all getting ready – all very exciting. Rubber suits are going on with talc and being finished on top with a dash of oil. Wear rubber and you will sweat buckets. I had gone to a hard-core gay S&M, gear mfrs. in town – all gas masks and body-bags-uurghh! I asked the guy to make me a pink crop top and mini. He looked at me reluctantly, but he took the business.
>
> Make-up starts going on and setting-powder was thick in the air. J would get out the sparkling white and pizza (the only things I ever saw in the fridge).
>
> Then we would all get in a limo and arrive in style at the venue. (It can be cheaper than multiple taxis to hire a limo and it makes the night very special – you used to see the West End full of them with hens screeching out of the windows). We could do two nights in a

row 'til four in the morning. We had a great time on the scene and did all the big parties and yearly specials. The only one I missed was the Sex Maniacs' Ball. I don't think I missed much there; Miss Thierry gave me a very drab account of a visit there which included: a bored looking girl giving an old guy a suck and a piece of plastic sheeting, hung up, which people pressed against, feeling each other through it; not so crazy and we may need to re-use this idea now with Covid!

At one big party (Mass at Brixton I think) Jack or Angie, whispered in my ear that a young couple wanted to talk to me in the bogs. I went for the meet and they wanted to take me home with them. She was very cute: quite a babe, and liked a good whipping on the cross. She had quite a bit of bruising from the night – the BDSM scene always made me squirm a bit. They wanted to play a bit and he was bi-curious. So we went back to their flat. It was a bit awkward in a way, but we ended up having some spunky fun, he got a first suck – and to bed and away in the morning.

The thing about the whole liberated scene is that (in case you, the casual and non-libertine reader, are going to start writing to your MP in a blazing torrent of indignation): It is all about consenting adults, having some fun in a safe environment, away from the public gaze. Most people on the scene are very well-behaved and only want to have some fun in the venue and then go home, back to normal life. Many couples join the scene to spice things up a bit. For others it is their only sexual outlet. When you get talking to people you realise there is a proper scene: people know people and recognize faces (or other parts) and you talk about all the clubs and what they are like and where people last went. A few people are 'lifestyle' and they run associated businesses or go to parties or clubs each week and look a bit counter-culture even in daytime.

The venues are usually fairly bland from the outside, there is not much of a clue as to what is going on inside and attendees do not hang about outside. There are usually strict 'no drugs or prostitution' policies and anyone who looks drunk or starts getting leery at others in that annoying way or touching after the polite 'no', will soon be chucked out. (See appendix 2)

Chapter 8
Chariots

CHARIOTS, LIVERPOOL STREET, WAS THE BIGGEST GAY SAUNA IN LONDON. I landed a Sunday job there. I had put my name down ages ago and they rang on a Saturday, obviously desperate. The Sunday shift inevitably turned into a full-time job. It was a fabulous community there and I made friends – even the sort of friends who you would associate with outside, which is rare at work. I would bump into them in Old Compton Street or at Heaven. It was close-knit community – both staff and customers – though most visitors took on the mantle of Mr. Anonymous; they came, they saw, they conquered, then slipped back out again into the hum of the city.

There was a 'character' working there. He was known as 'Sarge' and it was rumoured that he was ex-police; he drove a police-esque Landrover; but no-one was exactly sure. His job in Chariots, was apparently, 'maintenance'. I think I once saw him glue a tile down somewhere. Apart from that, he would give me a right-thorough feel-up in the steamer – which I totally enjoyed and he would spin volumes of bullshit to us newer staff members. He was one of those nice characters you never forget. When he gave me my induction there, he said, "this job'll put 'airs on yer' chest me'laddo".

Chariots (enthusiastically sub-headed – 'Roman Spa') was owned by straight people (who kept out of sight) and Chariots had two other smaller satellites. I went to the Streatham one a few times and it was small and intimate. It was a boring-job at Chariots, but in-between duties, I could pop in the steamer and have a mouthful, or cruise around the cabins in my little shorts and get rushed into some action. Liverpool Street had a huge Romanesque plunge-pool which was very up-scale for the time. The walls and pillars were painted with *tromp-l'oeil* in marble-esque-Romanesque. They also had a restaurant/bar next door, open to the general public, so we often carried food back into the sauna for customers who ordered, thereby slipping outside into the real world for a few minutes.

It was a strange sort of job. You were working in a very 'off-road' atmosphere. It sometimes seemed very unreal. It was a whole sub-cult of a sub-cult. I sometimes wondered if passers-by in the side street outside had any inclination of what the place was. It was only ten minutes from Liverpool Street station. The customers came and went. I often felt jealous of some of them we got to know, having 'proper' jobs in the 'real' world and doing something productive. But then they would look at us and think that we were lucky to be working where they came for pleasure and that we had none of their worries. It must be the same thing when you are a gym instructor, or working in a restaurant, or being a holiday rep; you feel that the customers are normal and you are in a weird unreality.

I worked with a young Turkish lad, Os, at the bar upstairs and with several others; some had been working there since it opened. It was too easy to keep turning up. Sid was from south of the equator somewhere; he was a comedian and he was classically good looking: he had a face from a 1970s Malboro cigarette advert, though slightly Italianate rather than American; I often wondered what the xxxx he was doing working here, when he could have done anything with that face. Ron, one of the duty managers, was apparently an ex-soap star from Portugal and another was a professional hairdresser; again what the hell were they doing? Easy cash and regular work.

I was often paired at the bar with a young French guy, Florent. He once said, with an intelligent smile, 'that this had to be the worst job he ever had'. He still enjoyed it and I do not think that his next job, in sales, was nearly as much mind-numbing fun.

Saturday evenings was the 'muscle-Mary parade' – all the bodybuilders and escorts promenaded around the place before going out clubbing; towels tightly wrapped and a purposeful walk like 'you may watch but don't touch unless you are the chosen few'. They never appealed to me anyway. I liked the old guys as they treated you like a princess and a xxxx is a xxxx in the miasma of steam and heat.

I once remember a young guy came into the steamer, went a bit wild and was in a good mood and all of a sudden it was mayhem; it looked like a scene from a porn film orgy; it lasted for about ten minutes but you will remember it forever.

I never saw a T-girl in there, but this was before all the saunas started 'T-girl and admirer' days. As it was 'men only' I do not even know if a well-presented T-girl or trans person with implants (still male officially) would have even got in – that would have been interesting. Tranny/T-girl days are usually specific days or times at saunas; some allow them in any time; but some gay guys do not like trannies, so it can clash – hence the 'T-girl days', then everyone knows what to expect.

One day, a 'new-boy' was introduced at the bar upstairs. Amazingly, he stated that he was NOT gay. This was beyond belief. Why would a straight lad want to work in a gay orgy? He was very nice and did his job. No-one said boo to him – we let him be. He never deviated or engaged in anything. Maybe he was doing research for a thesis or something.

One afternoon, we were all in a good mood and I met a few of the Chariots' staff at Heaven club much later on – it was strange seeing such a large posse from Chariots together at Heaven. I was dressed. Steve, a huge, very good-looking work pal, was amazed and could not keep his big muscular hands off me. I once saw my university lecturer at Chariots. He was a big cheese in certain circles of academia, but his sexuality was well-known. He went deep purple, seated in his lounger by the pool when he spotted me at the bar – but I reassured him and we were cordial. He had nothing to worry about. Chariots, Liverpool Street, is no more. They sold the plot for re-development.

Chapter 9
Stunners

BEFORE ALL the swingers' clubs and gay saunas started doing T-girl days, there was Stunners club. It was in the Cable Street Studios which was an old block turned into business units.   Jayne, the organiser, had rented out a suite and some adjoining space over the cobbles for a lovely appendage café. At two in the morning you could get a smoked salmon sandwich and chat to friends, before going back in the main club's boudoirs and playrooms for another six mouthfuls.

It was like a sports event: prepare; go; see how many you can do. The admirers were all sorts. They were allowed to wear street clothes but 'make an effort'. This does look better than guys in towels in the saunas which is never very flattering. How about nice bathrobes? Surely that is more flattering? The guys at Stunners loved me. There were, no doubt, a few famous people dotted about dressed up but under all that make-up you would never know.

On my first visit, a young tranny showed me about – not that there was much point as the club was tiny, with about four rooms and a small dance floor and bar, but at clubs they like to show you about first; I suppose then there are no miss-understandings.   Ahhh! The smell of bleach and spunk...I was home. I had many fab nights at Stunners. I avoided the mixed nights which were more for general swingers. I find that when you get mixed nights, the whole dynamic changes and all of a sudden there are rules: 'couples only here', 'only two in this room at a time'...When it is men only there are fewer rules and everyone seems to behave.

Stunners club was also very sociable and a great meeting point. It was a sort of trans-community centre where you could also have unlimited raunchy fun and leave at three in the morning feeling like you had had enough, for now. When Jayne died, the club came to a halt and no-one managed to carry it on and then the site was redeveloped.

I still find some who remember Stunners and say, "I probably saw you there once Tra-ycee, in fact I am sure ....."

Chapter 10

Europe and the international T-scene, help!

I ONCE DID THE SPARTACUS TOUR. *Spartacus* was the gay Europe guidebook. I went long before the Euro. Europe was very cheap and a lot of fun then. In every town you turned up in, the first thing was to find, after a hostel, the 'gay map' then you check out all the bars and saunas. I also met a young Swedish woman I went around with in Barcelona for a few days, doing the sights. I ended up in Sitges after Barcelona, via Amsterdam and Rome. I was 'Inter-railing' but on the buses. The European tour; a rite of passage like the grand tour of old; and with as much debauchery as its nineteenth century grandmother.

In Sitges, I met a couple of strange characters. (I was in male mode here). The young lad spoke good English, had a beautiful, bronzed, toned body, a mop of golden curls and was wearing a green thong. He was seated at the bar. His friend, Didier, was an older guy: slim, very handsome face, perfect teeth and a good tan. Didier picked me up from a beach bar. He took me to the local sauna. He appeared to be 'living' in a local hotel. It turned out that they were both alcoholics and that was a great shame. They seemed like refugees from the real world and I fancied that Didier was the black sheep of an aristocratic family, consigned to spend his days improving his tan while existing on a small allowance, living in a cheap hotel in a tourist town, picking up visitors in summer as sport.

Rome was hot in summer. Most locals move out for summer. McDonald's offered respite as it had air-conditioning. It also offered good coffee and provided some other local specialities, being in Rome – and this was long before all branches started serving better coffee and specialities.

Rome was a bit cruisy. There were a few clubs dotted about, but no gay village. Everywhere you walked, crumbled walls and ancient ruins shimmered in the heat. The Romans were not wrapping it all up in cotton wool: beer bottles littered the *Circus Maximus* and bits of ruin poked out everywhere open to anyone. It was so hot that you could walk about at night wearing practically nothing. I checked out all the gay bars and clubs, there did not seem to be that many; nothing like the London scene. Rome has a beach (not in the city centre) but a short train journey away – at Ostia. The sand-dunes were cruisy with action and I saw a group of transsexuals on the beach, sitting having a picnic.

All the clubs in Europe at this time had this strange lighting in them which made you glow. They all had darkrooms at the back – something we do not have here. You have not lived until you have been in the darkrooms of the Cockring in Amsterdam. I met a young guy, Daniel, from the Seychelles in a bar in Warmoesstraat, the leather and fetish epi-centre – we went to one of the Thermos saunas – which were vast. While there, I saw a flyer, and a day later got on a special bus to a big out of town fetish party in a big warehouse. It was madness.

I did not see much in the way of drag – anywhere. I was not looking for it particularly. I strongly suspect that against all the odds, the UK is the best place in Europe for dragging up. I have tried finding out about Berlin and cannot seem to find anything – I thought that would be a mecca.

Further afield, New York, of course, would be a different proposition and has a drag history, including revolution by drag queens and recently, Wigstock. (Can we not get together and charter a plane and go one year?) I have not met one tranny who has ever mentioned it and some trannies really get about.

I wonder if any trannies or T-girls went to Tangier in its hey-day when it was full of ex-pat-homos, writers, artists and eccentrics; the Tangerinos. From what I have read, Tangiers was more about native rent-boys living off sugar daddies than an exuberant drag or a flamboyant scene.

People have murmured that Benidorm is great for dressing up. I find that unless you actually go to a place and check it out first-hand with your own eyes, you do not know for sure about anything and you inevitably find that most of the prior information you had was bogus – even in this age.

I would welcome a bit more information on dragging up around the world and the various scenes. I good guidebook (a real book and not a collection of half-baked, out of date websites) would be useful. Someone will tell me it exists. If not, let us go round the world in drag and write it up. Contact me if you can fund my trip.

Ps: I have been told a number of times that Benidorm is worth it. A friend went to Israel and dressed, but said to stick to Tel-Aviv and avoid religious areas.

Chapter 11
More out and about

T-GIRL DAYS AT THE CLUBS ARE GREAT. They are also social events; you always bump into people you know, girls and admirers – and they are all over the UK. Most clubs have separate T-girl changing, so the guys only see you dressed. Sit in the coffee shop and shut your eyes; there is a conversation going on about diesel engines or drill bits....it could be any bar/pub/office in Britain...except, eyes open and everyone is made-up, nails painted and wearing dresses.

Trannies come from all walks of life. There are many professionals and highly skilled people – and at least 50% are ex-military, ex-kick-boxers or martial arts people and many seem to race motorbikes.... Some are pretty tasty, so 'watch ya, mouf' with T-girls, as they can change back into man-mode quickly. Many turn up to the same clubs each week and it is normal weekly life. One club provides a great cooked lunch as part of the entrance fee. Lunch is an occasion, everyone stops what they are doing and they come down to the buffet. I would dress up with a bit more glam for lunch – where else can you do that? Some have bars, coffee shops, lounges and all of the usual sauna, steam-room stuff separate from all the cabins and fun rooms; which can cover a vast area...it is a great day out. All they need is a nail bar, clothes and shoe shopping, make up counters, a hotel on-site and you would have a proper emporium. I thought of it first. (01.01.21).

Many have to hide this part of their lives away which is sad. They hire a locker at a club and have to scrub every scrap of nail varnish off before leaving. Many turn up to socialise. On this scene, you do not have to do anything you do not want to; or you can choose to get pillaged by three hunks and enjoy a good spit-roasting or be on your knees for hours. A hot T-girl can have queues outside a cabin. I once had to beg to be let out to get a cup of tea as more were streaming in for a turn. It is the stuff of fantasies.

The clubs are a great safety valve for letting off a bit of steam. They are totally inconspicuous from the outside and there is never any trouble (very rare). They are a safe place. You will not get attacked, I have never yet heard of an incident – like some have had while cruising or dogging. Hence they cause nobody any bother. So why tighten up on them or get all prudish about it? (It is like the swingers and the BDSM scene – in fact, there are frequent cross-overs on these scenes). It all happens with consenting adults and a strict 'no drugs' policy – apart from poppers which are considered normal. Usually there are free condoms and lube about and community literature – some even have HIV testing days. There are too many grey areas (I am writing this during the 2020 Covid time so there is now no safe area) but in normal times always wear a rubber for A. O is different for many. Much lower risk anyway. Many are now on PRED and bare-backing, but always check things as it is easy in a big group to lose track of things. Boswell went 'armoured' to the Strand for pickups – he still got gonorrhoea.

There are plenty of non-sex events. Some are not in it for the sex! There are plenty of clubs, social clubs and big events like 'Sparkle' in Manchester Village in the summer. "It is our day today" as my favourite drag queen, Thorini, said while DJing during Sparkle weekend. The atmosphere in the village is electric on Sparkle weekend.

> I remember two years back, T-friendly bars packed with fab people till four or five in the morning. Stalls and shows in the park in the day. Hot sunshine in Canal Street gently melting make-up; coffee at tables; friends popping by; escapism and freedom from the normal world. Some, on their first time out and nervous as hell are looked after by others. There are a couple of websites that link it all together now and usually people ask, "you on X or Y?" (Get some cards printed to give out with your username).

Although Pride marches and events are great fun and a good excuse to dress up, I think Pride needs to go back to its roots as a protest march. Peter Tatchell has written about this. LGBTQ+ rights and issues get scant mention during Pride. If Pride was more political, about ascertaining rights and freedoms, and we could still wear a pink thong to march that would be perfect. (See appendix 3)

> Jaydee and I strolled into Leeds town centre at about ten in the morning hoping to join the march. Of course, you need to register six months prior to do that. Anyway, after running around trying to get through the massive cordon of railings which snaked around the whole centre (we must have covered half the town and Jaydee was nearly going to murder me) we ended up at a pelican crossing with a gap – no railings – and we stood still. All of a sudden the flag, leading the parade, was under our noses and there were two vacant spaces. As we were 'dressed' we easily slipped in and grabbed a piece of the side seam each and helped to carry the flag into town! We walked about three miles too; the heels held up and the light shower did not mess up our outfits. When we reached the town centre

again we parted company and joined the general melee around the Viaduct and had a drink in a bar. There were about 20,000 people in town for Pride apparently.

There is still homophobia and trans-phobia, originated by many people who should know better – and who themselves complain of discrimination. That is why Pride is still needed, whatever it has morphed into. It is only one day a year. If you do not like it stay away from town for that day only; like I do when there is a football match on. Straight sexuality is in your face 24/7: in advertising, in the media, arts and in the streets, so LGBTQ+ for a day? In any case, no-one is having sex in the streets during Pride. If anyone has a problem with Pride happening, they are paying *way too* much attention to it all.

Chapter 12
Hassle, clothes-phobia and trans-phobia. Why?

IF YOU DRESS UP (IN ANY WAY THAT IS SLIGHTLY DIFFERENT TO THE BLAND NORM WHERE YOU LIVE, WHICH IS USUALLY VERY BLAND (UNLESS YOU ARE LUCKY ENOUGH TO BE A GUARDS' OFFICER OR YOU ARE ON THE TELLY) OR YOU GO OUT IN PUBLIC LOOKING A BIT 'INTERESTING' at some point you will get anything from strange looks to a mouthful of bile from some low-life in the street.

When in drag I have had my share of abuse. I have always been curious as to why this happens. I am going to try to analyse it. I think more open discussion would drill down into the true causes of hate. Then we can deal with it.

If I pass someone in a public place or at a private gathering and they look a bit different or eccentric, I do not open my cake-'ole and start yelling at them or cussing as I walk past or even tittering, which is worse; as a laugh is more expressive than any words.

If T-girls or drag queens get abuse, it is usually of a homophobic or trans-phobic nature– ninety-nine per cent. The cat-calls or growls are not limited to: "hey you, why do you dress up as a bird?"

I always wished I could have interrogated all these abusers properly. "Why are you spouting this?" "What is your problem with someone dressing or appearing to be different from the masses or yourself (yourself as the presumed gold-standard)?" "Why are you so affected by it and why do you need to open your big fat mouth about it or even tut and shake your head?"

What if a drag queen, CD or tranny, gets homophobic abuse in the street, but is happily married and straight? What is the supposed justification for the abuse then? The abuser should be very happy that their objection to anything gay, if that is the intent, is unfounded as the CD whilst being 'eccentrically' dressed up, may have produced children and is populating the planet – as we often suppose there is a 'religious' or 'you are not populating the planet' based motive for homophobic abuse. How does an abuser know the exact sexuality of someone based on their outward appearance? If they knew that the CD they had screamed at, had produced children, or even had grandchildren, would that pacify them? Would they still hate the CD simply because of the way they were dressed, wearing make-up and 'women's-wear'?

Is our abuser afraid that if the visual difference between the sexes is blurred, *they* may make a mistake? Is this actually likely? So what if they do? Apparently, in Poland, you can get killed for looking trans. Such is the hatred for anyone who transgresses norms – but who are the normal people? This kind of social paranoia is the sure sign of a primitive, simple-minded people or society.

Leaving aside pure homophobia now, if a T-girl gets homophobic abuse and they *are* gay or bi-sexual, and something has aroused the suspicion of this possible fact, what is the reasoning for the abuse now? Without knowing the content of the abuse, which is usually incoherent and shows a low mental age – why is the abusive person bothered about their victim's sexuality? What difference does sexuality and appearance make; if men want to feminise (whatever that commonly implies) themselves or women want to appear more masculine? Why do men have to be masculine and vice-a-versa? Who defines what masculinity is? What does heterosexuality achieve anyway – that it must be so guarded and upheld at all times as the sacred norm?

What is the cause of resentment directed at those who are identified rightly or wrongly as being homosexual or trans? Why are the abusers so concerned if a small minority of our population want same-sex relationships or want to subvert normal gender stereotypes or dress differently? No one is forcing the hater to watch gay sex all day, wear a dress (if male) or join in gay or other bohemian or sub-culture activities. Even if 'gayness' or 'dressing up' and subverting gender stereotypes, becomes popular, there will always be men who want to have sex with women. We are not exactly short of people on the planet either, unless your own tribe is vanishing and you think it is worth preservation – others may disagree – and think you are better off dying out.

Some trans/homosexual haters are educated people and run countries. This is all the more perplexing; for educated or worldly people to 'hate' with no sound justification if they are not affected directly to their own detriment by the people they hate.

Illogical hatred is the cause of all the friction in the world and causes ethnic cleansing, wars and un-just subjugation of certain groups of society. The reasons given for hatred of: open displays of trans culture; wearing gender-blurring clothes (not gender-neutral); or gayness (that is not having sex on the streets, but behaving as straight people do with a partner in public, like holding hands); are usually that it will lead to 'a breakdown in society and a breakdown of moral behaviour'. How will it do that and to whom? Is your society that fabulous and perfect that a few drag queens or same-sex couples are going to tarnish the whole thing, invoke the wrath of the devil or turn your state into a banana republic and reduce your GDP by half? Those things probably apply already and you are using scapegoats.

We all know what I am trying to boil it down to. The big 'why'? Many, even in our permissive society, do *not* like the idea of gay sex (or any appearance of 'gayness' which includes men wearing dresses) and that usually is limited to men; though many lesbians get extreme harassment too. Why?

If anyone says "gay stuff is in my face all the time" – i.e. any more than heterosexual sexuality is already in our faces in the media, film and arts then they are probably taking too close a look at gay stuff. One lesbian kiss on Brookside and there were questions in the Commons and a national furore.

Fear of someone or a group is usually cited as a reason for hatred. I think this is slightly optimistic. It may be that it is a more an apprehension of a 'different group' whom are upsetting someone's cherished beliefs and value systems; putting a spanner in their works. Educated people should look at something, analyse it and think: "It does not affect me – nothing to do with me" and walk on. Many educated people seem to retain their subjective 'uneducated' thought patterns and mutter about trans, blurring of norms, dressing-up or homo-stuff, as it is something they do not understand. Parts of my family are highly educated and travel widely, but they mix within in a very small group of people and rarely venture out of that zone.

> One night on the way to a fetish party, we were all in high spirits with J & A and the regular posse. We all trouped through Leicester Square and were dressed up, for a laugh, on the way to the party. I knew it would happen. The lead couple comprising J & A; J, wearing leather chaps with butt cheeks on show, (I have to admit – which though not illegal by any means, could have had a legitimate 'tut' from an outraged passing Zealot, I would have not been bothered with) but J & A got a load of homophobic abuse from some git. But J & A were straight.

How does that balance? Guilty by association or by wearing forbidden clothes? Trans or gay-hating is a very complex phenomena. We need to understand the 'why' then we can start to combat it through education.

Chapter 13
Out of town again

CORPORATE PARTIES AND NIGHTCLUBS IN TOWN were starting to get a bit dull and frankly depressing. I needed a change!

In those early internet days, I had a request by email: "could I attend a party? Paid, of course". It was a job. It was at Hampton Court Palace, the Georgian House, to be exact – which is hired out for events. The party transpired to be that of a London courier company. I took Miss Thierry, partner of choice, as she made a grand effort and we could rely on each other – and we did not do drugs, which made most queens in town totally unreliable and flaky (pot does that especially and cocaine turns them into jackasses), which you do not want when you are an entertainer on a job.

We started on our adventure. When we turned up, I still half expected it to be a wind-up. At the front door, we were pointed to the right building, to our relief.

While we were upstairs changing – it was all very well laid on for us – some girls (real girls, as we always term them) bought some water up for us and of, course, they were curious. Everyone was in that excitable, party mood. I remember a small group lingering at the back of the room and amongst all the activity and doing make-up with Miss T, my eye caught one of them.

We had a great time; it was a very nice house; people were all over it, in the kitchen and upstairs. It was all strangely erotic – and a stupor of fun and desire permeated the house. I changed into something more comfortable. At some point I noticed the girl again...something happened...stuff happened .....

We have been together now for twenty years.

Chapter 14
Sexuality

TED MORGAN (the name is an anagram) wrote the lengthy tome of Somerset Maugham's biography [phew, when you finish that one]. Ted Morgan did not understand bi-sexuality in my opinion. Maugham and Syrie Wellcome (later Maugham) had a child and were married. Maugham had 'gay sex-frolics' with an older man when he was very young. When older he was into men exclusively it would seem. What this means is that Somerset was bi-sexual. *Not* gay and pretending to be straight. How can you have sex with a woman if you do not like it, even for a day or a minute or for many years? Some could say that Somerset was actually gay and he must have shut his eyes during sex or pretended Syrie was a man....I find all this pretty unlikely and that kind of relationship would end in a week unless there were vast sums of money involved. It has been estimated that a huge part of the population are actually bi-sexual, in different stages; this is a far more likely scenario.

What happens with a bi-sexual over life? It may end up with gravitating more to one or to the other, or even to trans people (that's put a spanner in there for you). This will explain how male celebrities who were married or living heterosexual lives – now 'come out' as gay to a tumult in the press. They are actually bi-sexual. It means that they like men and they like women (or did like women or did like men) but now they like men or women (or in-betweens) more. Freud said that the libido can oscillate between preferences during life. Additionally, if the total libido dips, then the lesser preference may even vanish, which is a neat theory. Many cannot accept that bi-sexuality exists or they think it is some kind of perversion. Never mind coffee-cionados (quoting from advertising now); we are *all* 'perverts' now.

As you may have wondered, I am bi-sexual, so that qualifies me to make this commentary.

Chapter 15
Trannying and Dragging up: Ten Top Tips that could save you heaps of time and trouble; learn from my mistakes.

IF YOU WANT TO START DRAGGING UP or trannying about town here are some top tips for starting out:

Join one of the popular website communities. TV-Chix is the best, in my opinion. It has a nice layout and is more than just a 'looking for sex' site. You will find lots of advice, forums and event listings.

But go out and do it or the whole thing makes no sense. You could do it all on the internet... but to never go out and taste that excitement and smell the bars, the streets and the hotch-potch of people and characters you will meet... or what is life for? (This is written during the Covid lockdowns of 2021, so who knows if we will ever get out again, but...) There are many clubs and events and parties. Drag is becoming less shocking now to straights, though you still need to be careful and remember there is a 'time and a place' (usually us being on the telly for straights) despite our grand ideals of hard-won equality and notions of freedom – which is a big porky. Some are more equal than others and if you step around the wrong corner wearing a skimpy top and a pink scarf...

Here are ten top tips which may save you time and mistakes – even if you do one thing, it is worth me spending the time on it for you.

First: Shaving and tanning.

GET A CLOSE FACE SHAVE. This will be the closest shave of your life: go up and down and back again, hold taught and go over slowly. With all the complex products out there, a simple twin-blade and hotel shampoo does the job perfectly and simply. You should wax your back, wax or shave legs, arms and armpits, also chest and even the fingers. I was once up-braided for not shaving my armpits, before a quiz show filming. It was a stupid oversight. I actually prefer to be shaved anyway. If you always shave your pits, you can never be caught out, as that is very easy to forget for some reason!

Tip: when shaving your legs, go easy. It is very easy to nick yourself around the outer sides of the knee joint. Take it steady. Use plenty of soap or gel, keep rinsing off cut hair and after taking off a mass, rinse the blade. Go over each section a few times, getting more off. When done, dry off, lie on the bed and you will see you have missed bits. You can do these dry or with a bit of moisturiser. Watch the backs of your legs; it is easy to miss whole sections you cannot see easily. While you do all this, you may as well do some crevices too, especially if you wear skimpy stuff. Many shave cock and balls. This takes practice. Best to start with some electric clippers (be careful) to take huge clumps off and not block the razor; that works in general too for legs and armpits. It may not show, but knowing you are not a hairy monkey underneath can work wonders for confidence. Viz-a-viz: French women who always wear nice underwear.

Always put loads of moisturiser on after any shaving to calm it all down (except the face or makeup may slide off). Olive oil works well on legs and will give a slight tint in the absence of fake tan. If you tan first, you may 'shave off' some tan, but tanning after shaving can sting a bit. The tan sometimes needs a few days of re-applying to even out, sort out missed patches and build to a reasonable colour. San Tropez was the one, but we bought some brilliant 'tanning liquid in an eyedropper bottle with pipette' (which you then add moisturiser to and mix in your palm or a small tub), from QVC, (which is easy to shop from as you can send it back if you do not like it, even if you have used it!)

After all that shaving or de-hairing and tanning you can wear skimpy outfits and not have to hide under layers of clothing. I do not think it is aesthetic to have body-hair sticking out all over the place, but in terms of 'freedom' you could argue that it does not matter and that you can't have a tranny uniform or we are back to scratch. There is a sort of tranny uniform that has emerged (and that goes for drag queens too). I am often the only queen in the bar in a pink dress – surrounded by so much black you would think we are at a funeral.

Second: Body and health:

We once dropped into Escape Bar, in Soho, as a novelty, with Miss Thierry and my new partner (real girl). My partner being unfazed by it all, after visiting a bookshop and quite happy, we hung about with a drink. Pete Burns was by the bar all done up. The one thing we noticed was that s/he did not seem to have much posture or grace – this is something you need to cultivate when dressed up if you want the accepted drag queen image; you cannot slouch about like a bloke or walk like a donkey. Body and health all contribute to this and will improve your look dramatically.

The point of this chapter is this to try and help you by looking at my failures. When I am out in Tracy mode, many people say to me: (and that means when I was last out before the first Covid lockdown, which is early 2020): "How do you get *this* body? How can you look *so* good? Are you full time? How come you are so skinny and so toned? I can't answer all that in a noisy bar, but I wish I could place my hands on someone's head (Spock-style) and impart the following:

I was always naturally slim and had a slim neck, wrists and ankles (which makes me look odd in the real world and all my life I have had comments such as: 'nooo...you're too skinny...I would put on some weight if I were you....too skinny for a bloke...', or I get snarled at like I am a freak or not normal. As Tracy, my status is at the top for a change. I was very sporty in my own way (outdoor sports); not to bore you too much with all that, but I toned up when young and have always dabbled in weight training (slow gainer; skinny-toned look) and, even now, I look for any excuse to process firewood or do something physical. I am 5'9", size 8 feet and no Adam's apple to speak of. Okay, I have some good genetics for drag, but a while back, while running my own business for ten years, I did get out of shape for the first time. Too much desk and too much junk food creep. One day, I said, "enough"; get the Atkins book out again, cut the junk (not like we are short of good food anyway in our house) and get out on bike/run/weights again. I did.
On a holiday, I used the place as a fitness camp, went to all the classes and the gym and managed to keep ahead of all the young bucks. I carried on when back. We had another holiday there and I did the same, so this is about two years' process. I think I lost...about fifteen-plus kilos and went from (a tight) thirty-four waist back down to the twenty-eight I had always been. I did it. I have clothes in the loft which wrap around me twice. Exercise is only about 20% of it. Diet is the main thing or rather, the eating style or regime. With the best of these plans you can stick with them for life as they do not place any importance in cutting calories or fat (the right type of fat that is).

Surgical procedures are not within the scope of this book. I know a TV, (a surgeon) who has written an excellent book on bariatric procedures. Diet is discussed as a first option. I have not had any surgery done on any counts (not yet!) and prefer the natural look. I did try laser hair removal, it all grew back again. A face lift would be my only thing; I do not need it yet, but I can see the point of a tiny tuck as you get older. I suppose surgery gets addictive and then you end up looking very odd. However, getting back to food, here *is* something that I know about.

After thirty years of reading up on diet, nutrition and doing sports; here is the nub of it: *Cut the carbs* (unless you are training for six hours a day). If you are in training, check out the classic, *Paleo Diet for Athletes*, by L. Cordain and J. Friel. Normal folk: immediately cut foods such as: bread, grains and potatoes; and cut sugar; ban fake-food and junk-food and use the glycaemic index (refined to glycaemic-load) to your advantage. The weight will slide off. Note: kids can eat anything and get away with it, but when they hit thirty, years of neglect will start taking a toll. Even fruit and veg. has carbs, so you will need to be consuming under 50g a day of carbs to be safe to start with. Atkins starts you on 20g, which is like one apple or a banana or three broccoli florets. Count carbs, not calories and you will win.

There is nothing you can do about ageing. You can make the best of it and still give the young queens a run for their money. If you are young and start right now you may keep like that for ever. Look after your skin, eat well and start on the polyphenols now. Olive oil (extra virgin), cacao powder, alpha-linolenics (walnuts), oily fish twice a week at least (tin of sardines does the job), fruit and veg – and cut down on lectins. There is enough info out there now on all this. I started with Atkins years ago and the book is a mine of information still to this day; new guru Dr. Gundry is interesting re: lectins; and *The Paleo Diet* and the *Blood-Type Diet* are all essential reading.

A year or two can see huge changes. I did it. With something as simple as the paleo style of diet/Akins, you will not go far wrong. I am the living evidence that many minor ailments will totally disappear. I have not taken an Omeprazole or painkillers for years and the rough skin on the back of my arms vanished. Many other minor ailments that were building up receded or vanished. I have also binned copious amounts of packets of pills and potions that that were prescribed for my burgeoning list of petty ailments.

Cutting out junk-food or fake food is the start (and will solve most of your problems) and this can make a huge difference very quickly – but that is hard to start doing. Anything 'junk' contains strange ingredients and dodgy stuff that you would not easily find in your kitchen. Another category of junk-food also contains: flours, starches, sugars and oils (high in omega 6s) and dreaded trans fats that you do not need – most of all that will go straight on as fat – or poison you gradually over the years and leave you with a host of medical conditions (not hereditary, congenital, trauma related or viral).

Top tip: If you have cravings all the time for crisps (I was on a packet a day; they are vile and are basically poisonous)...get the deep-fat-fryer out again; fill with extra virgin olive oil (known as EVOO) and a block or two of lard (which is back in fashion). Slice up a couple of parsnips (high glycaemic, so have only after exercise or gardening or gym or chopping firewood); finely slice (2-4mm), throw in the hot oil; fry till browned (five minutes on high); no need to par-boil first; then no need to pat dry as EV olive oil is good for you; serve hot or cold, sprinkled with garlic salt, sprinkle of sea salt (no junky ketchup) or make a caper/garlic/mayo-mix spread to dip if you want. (Hellman's full-fat is the better of evils here). = No need for crisps anymore and 100x healthier than factory-made, fake-food-junk like Pringles which are addictive. You soon rid yourself of these addictions when you get used to real food again.

Once you are where you need to be; weight-wise or look-wise, you can have a few treats here and there until symptoms or weight reappears. Other tips I have learnt to save cash and your health:

Avoid any eating out anywhere or using restaurants. Chefs and commercial cooks are wholesale committed to putting flour and sugar in *everything*; and they delight in using cheap oils; top-heavy in omega 6s polyunsaturated fats (omega 3 is the good one); all this is basically poisoning us slowly. Any baked, made-up, hot or cold products: pies/pastries/pizzas will have dodgy oils in them (omega 6 top-heavy) or even worse trans-fats, which are borderline illegal. Cooks also like to use nightshades; they even use them raw and un-peeled like tomatoes and peppers (which are lectin bombs) *in everything*. Avoid jacket potatoes like the plague, apart from being high glycaemic, the skins are reputedly loaded with saponins and could be quite toxic; plants seem to concentrate their toxins in the skins or peels, a natural defence system against predators. They can be cooked-out, but why take any chances? We do not need to eat this stuff.

I now pass people queuing outside food outlets or doughnut shops and I cannot believe it; they may as well be eating rat poison. How easy is it to prepare a few simple things at home and take them out with you?

If you are in a hurry: make a quick salad mix, (no nightshades), with a bit of feta or goat's cheese, (you can eat anything with cheese); include a hard-boiled egg (made by batch in advance on Sunday night to use in the week) any left-over chicken bits or other (paleo diet) approved morsels (no deli-stuff), or veggie alternatives if you need to; all with some EVOO at the bottom of a large plastic jar. Shake it all up when ready; so easy; *so* much better.

After you have got over your carbohydrate and junk-food addictions, you will be able to go hours without food too. I used to hit the cafes or McDonalds' in a hypo-glycaemic panic before appointments. Now all I need is a few walnuts or even an apple (medium glycaemic) to stave off any pangs. After many years, I have also come up with a secret breakfast that is a winner. I can go out on that (for a hill run) and come back and then only need to eat for nutritional purposes, not because I am bonking out or in a hypo. If your diet is right you should be able to go out for a good few hours and be fine, even longer. There are other benefits too which will be apparent.

This summer, we gathered a bumper crop of apples, many from local disused orchards. All that free, organic food is just lying on the floor; juicy, sweet apples by the bag-load. They will just about keep, wrapped in boxes for a few months (February and still eating them). A few of those a day will sort you out. If you live in the country there are tonnes of wild berries and produce to be had (just do not pick by someone's front door).

Not many have the discipline to make changes of such magnitude, (swapping Pringles for apples) but the paleo-style/low-carb-style is much, much easier to stick with long term. Powder diets, low-fat or calorie restrictive diets can work short-term but most people relapse eventually and put it all back on again; and they cannot ever lose the 'wheat belly'... as usually they are still eating wheat (erhumm!) Calorie restriction does not work. Well it does in the sense that you could say that, "I am going to drive everywhere at 20mph to save petrol". It will work, sort of, but you will not keep that up for long; and there are better solutions such as: emptying the boot of ballast, driving moderately, using other fuels, cleaning your spark plugs or buying a more economical car.

I am still trim after about three years: no gain apart from muscle and I am almost back where I was when I was twenty-five/thirty. I cannot buy men's wear in normal shops as I am a twenty-eight inch waist. I have to shop in youth stores – where at least I am not buying 'dad's jeans'. That is one other advantage of the process, you have to buy a whole load of new clothes; which is a great excuse to update your wardrobe slightly as most men seem to keep wearing what they had when they were thirty – for life. Getting back on topic, you will also be able to wear fab things in drag and get away with outrageous skimpy stuff.

[A musing on fried food and nutrition]. Let us look at this. The health authorities have scared us all shitless over the years about eating too much 'fried foods'. This is purely a smokescreen to hide the true culprit of all our NCDs: the carbohydrate industry. Of course, no government will take that industry on; too many jobs at stake: all those bakeries, pie-makers, cake factories and farmers selling cereal crops.

There is *NO* evidence at all that frying food, *per se*, is bad for you, nor the action of cooking in oil; that it changes the food to its detriment or lowers the oil or food quality – apart from maybe a tiny nutrient loss inherent in all cooking (that is why I drink the drained vegetable water). This nonsensical paranoia includes outrage at deep-fat frying, as well. However, no-one seems to bother getting steamed up about Mr Chef with his 'pan fried' this or that or the restaurant with a 'grill' which is usually a hot-plate (therefore frying).

What *is* the point – is *what* you are frying and *what oil* you are using. Extra virgin olive oil, with a high polyphenol count, can easily take 200 degrees. Forget smoke-point. If you fry a plain (no breadcrumbs or flour) piece of white fish at 180 or 200 (does anyone fry at higher?), what is the problem? None. Many say that deep-frying also seals the food before cooking. It is also a good way to get more olive oil into you; Dr Gundry would have to approve of that! Beware, 'air fryers'; it is a big con. They are simply tiny convection ovens. I sent ours back to QVC. Get your old deep-fryer out, clean all the terrible and poisonous soya or sunflower oils out of. Fill it with half EVOO and half lard (back in favour now as a non-toxic fat). This mix will last for many fries and the trans-fat build up is negligible.

Interesting also, is that 'dairy' seems to have a 'null effect' on heart disease. Keep to lower quantities and go for the Casein A2 types of milk and cheese (our original protein). Some fat in the diet will also slow the glycaemic reaction of any fruit or veg or traces of carbs in other stuff – even better. Cream is better than milk as cream has no carbs and it tastes great. According to the paleo gurus, seven eggs a week are no problem either.

Note: browse papers from the journals of the Am. Heart Assn. The abstracts or conclusions are fine for a general read.

How to Start and not fail.

With all new year resolutions and statements like: 'I'm going on a diet from next Monday/after the holiday/after the wedding/next month/Jan ...here is a tip. Forget arbitrary schedules. If you are going to do something DO IT RIGHT NOW. Why waste another day, or week or month, getting nowhere and poisoning yourself, or putting on more weight? If you cannot start *right now*, you will never start, or you will be too wound up by the deadline date, or you will be stuffing yourself with pastries or bread for a week beforehand to make the most of it while you can...why do that to yourself, why sabotage your first month's progress before you have even stared? Take all your rice and pasta, cook it up, leave out for the birds; same with the bread. We thread cheap doughnuts on a string with a small baton on the bottom and hang it from the bird feeding station.

Third: The make-up, especially the foundation.

PLEASE FORGET ABOUT WOMENS' FOUNDATION unless you have no facial hair or have had electrolysis. You need to purchase Kryolan Paint Sticks for your base or similar PanStick/TV Stick or Dermacolour. These are all a thick, matt paste in a large lipstick-type tube or a tub. The mix is made for professionals and the stage. Wipe it on direct from the stick and smooth the stuff in with a sponge, or piece of foam rubber (I cut up bits and keep in my make-up box); do not wipe it all off though! Then fix with copious translucent powder. A friend finds that some Kryolan fixing spray I bought worked very well as a finisher to gloop it all together. Some like to use a base under the foundation.

Do not over-moisturize or the slap may slip off. Some say... that a 'red' foundation under the main layer hides beard shadow. I have never tried it. Transformer used to say, "grind in that powder well, Miss Thang". If you have been lasered and it worked – then you can use girls' make-up, which is the same stuff, but thinned down with moisturisers.

The make-up industry is a huge swindle. Save bits and pieces – mix your own up from end-scraps or cut-offs – it all lasts for years, despite what the companies like to tell you. I do not think old make-up causes any problems with skin unless you share with others. I have only ever found minor irritation in my eyes and that is with new products.

> I was changing in a club and, a very nice T-girl who is a make-up artist, demonstrated a 'touch up' with a Kohl pencil with one of my eyebrows (I merely use my natural line which is slim and slightly plucked and usually exaggerate a bit on what I have naturally). I was staggered with the result from a few well-applied strokes with the pencil and I thought that, whether or not you liked all their ideas, you would learn a huge amount with one hour with a make-up artist.

Fourth: The clothes.

WOMENS' CLOTHES ARE ALL WRONG; unless you have had oil put in your hips and fake implants and your back shortened – especially regarding skirts and dresses. Buy a sewing machine and start making things. You can stitch two pieces of lycra together in a curvy shape – or use something you like, bought from a charity shop or pound shop as a pattern or guide – or buy bits and pieces and chop them up and alter them. If you can fix a boiler or do your brakes on your car, you can operate a sewing machine! Do not go near 'tranny shops' or dressing services (oops, there go my advertisers). They will make you look very dowdy. If you have no other option, then maybe use them but I never used such services.

In all fabric design, use yourself as a mannequin and pin, look, take-off, do some large tack-stitches, quickly un-pick, re-stitch – until it is right, then hammer down with a zig-zag, stretch stitch or ordinary stitch. Once you have a good design, you can make multiples in different colours and matching bags and accessories in the same fabric. I get a lot of compliments on dresses, "where did you get that?" I got bored of saying, "I made it" as they do not believe you. Best is to say it is from an exclusive shop in Mayfair or such-like or "I have a dress maker". Go about with some experienced and glamorous T-girls; you will learn far more watching them get ready in the hotel room and asking them questions. If you want to get into drag-dressmaking, you will have to mix with drag-queens as few trannies seem to stitch which I always find strange.

Fifth: Make a gaff to tuck your tackle in.

This is an essential item that many have asked me about in the past or wondered in amazement at my own version of. It is...

A SIMPLE FLAT V-SHAPE OF SEMI-STRETCHY FABRIC, side-seamed for rigidity. It flattens down your cock 'n' balls and is especially needed when you are wearing tight gear. The gaff fabric can be lycra – the thicker the better. It can be a single layer and white or black, a good neutral compromise (or other colours if any parts of it will show). Spaghetti strapping holds it all together – and in position (I use loops at the sides or put a fake bow in). At the back of this book are some basic instructions.

Rouleau: is fabric tubing and the best thing for the ties. Start by stitching a 5-7 mm seam, cut off the excess, close the end up with a row of stitching and pull inside out with a knitting needle. It takes practice, but these straps are the foundation for many outfits and accessories.

The tuck and putting it on. If you learn to tuck, you will not need three pairs of tights to hide your bulge.

Method:- Balls up slightly and tuck in any excess bits behind the fabric (balls do not need to go right into the cavities but they can do). Cock goes under and flat depending on your size. Pull all into place; it should all be nice and flat-ish. Tie the gaff's straps up at the sides in a bow which can be tricky to do all at once (or even easier stitch it all in place beforehand, so you pull it on like normal briefs or leave it all unfixed so it can be re-adjusted at will. It does need to be pulled tight around the waist/hips, so any device (like a small ring or buckle and/or a half-hitch) would work for that and can be re-adjusted if needed. Pull the waist strapping up high (that is why you do not make the back part too long) and it should all clamp up together and stay put for quite a while.

Do not spend silly money on a ready-made gaff: I have seen them advertised: they look like support pants and you can't wear skimpy outfits over them easily and show off more flesh. If you wear a loose skirt you can do a semi-tuck with tight pants or a thong; pull tight as possible. You can use a modified gaff with elasticated sides for loose wear or swimming trunks or similar thong, but your own invention will fit better and will be snugger and clamp all in place better.

Whichever system you go for, you need to keep an eye on it in the mirrors here and there. There is nothing worse than showing cock 'n' balls through a shiny, lycra dress. Matt fabrics do not show it so badly, also patterns are kinder.

When you have the gaff thing right, make a pattern quickly (trace around and cut a piece of card out) to keep, so you can easily make more of them. You will need spares. In fact, they roll up so small that you can keep a spare in a handbag easily. Always carry a safety pin in your handbag for an emergency repair to a side strap.

As with all dressmaking, allow for different stretches in different types of fabric. Fabrics usually have a warp (up and down) and a weft (right to left) stretch, one way usually has more stretch to it, or you can use the bias stretch (across ways). I try and make the stretchy part the long part and the not so stretchy way the cross-ways part to keep the flatness, but you need to try it out. Cut out the V-shape both ways out of the fabric and lay it down over your bits and see how it tucks it all in. It is such a tiny piece of fabric you can afford to waste scraps trying different cuts and shapes.

Sixth: Hair:

YOU MUST SPEND DECENT MONEY on your wig – minimum of £150 usually.

> The wig becomes a part of you. After make-up and putting the outfit on (carefully if over the head), then all the jewellery and any other accessories on... you still look unfinished. The moment that wig goes on, a huge transformation takes place. I have heard people gasp in amazement once this happens. You also get into proper character with it on. It is the one thing that makes the huge difference. It really does finish the whole thing off. You never take it off in front of anyone, apart from back at the hotel in your room with your room-sharer, not even other visiting T-girls. If you take it off, then you take off all the rest of it off as well and wash off. Girls (real) never take a wig off in public, so why should you?

I went through a few odd phases before I arrived at long and blond; it is always a winner. Put brown liner over your brows if needed (over a bit of foundation). Blond is a bit of a tranny uniform, but it works and you get noticed. I thought I could never go blond until one day I tried it; wow!

Wigs can be tricky to wear. If you adjust it with your hands while out, learn the correct motions, by practicing first. You may need hairspray to keep it in place (use proper wig spray and do not buy rubbish from dodgy wig shops selling £30 wigs). When putting it on start at the front then pull the back down. Make sure it is well seated and all straight. Do not pull it too far down the forehead like a cloth cap if you can help it. A wig cap is not needed if you have short hair. Have fun with colours; go mad like real girls do. Long wigs (to the mid-back) always look better to me. It is more hassle to keep tidy but is way more glam unless you have your own hair which can be any length. When out and about, take a brush with you (a mini-fold up type with mirror is good) as you can tidy it up periodically. If you step outdoors it *will* birds-nest in the slightest breeze in seconds.

The best places to buy wigs: from companies like Hot-Hair or Simply Wigs. I used to get a few wigs in Brixton Market. They were okay-ish. Although they lasted well, the cuts were not that nice and some were a bit lurid. There is a huge amount on the net about wig care, re-styling and using cheaper wigs and clever tips. Wash in lukewarm water; a bit of fabric conditioner can help; and get wig-dedicated sprays from the above mentioned only. Brush frequently, but there is no need to rip it to shreds with the brush or you will lose hair each time and damage the fibres. Start from the ends and tease it through until you can go for it. It is amazing what a quick brush will do at half time. At the other end of the spectrum, the club-kids and proper draggoes will get very creative and do things to their wigs that would send the Trendco rep into spasms.

Seventh: Shoes.

SIX INCH HEELS; They are not *that* sexy. They make you look too tall for a start (like seven foot) and your foot arches *will* fail eventually, like mine did. One day, walking about town in normal shoes I was in so much pain, I had to lean against the wall of DH Evans in Regent Street. I started wearing small heels and amazingly no-one noticed! I could run in them and I never had that terrible pain again. It still hurts whatever shoes you wear as the shoes are rubbing against bare skin and/or putting your foot in a very unnatural position. The alternative is to go totally draggo-tastic and make polystyrene platforms one foot tall like Miss Thierry and Burnel wore.

> We were once walking past the Raymond Revue bar in Soho, when a greasy-type, they used to have hanging about the entrance, hollered out, "hey, you. You walk like a horse, you will never make it!" Practise walking around the garden and on uneven ground and cobbles – or when you hit town you will be over like a shot. In kitten heels you should have no problems. During Sparkle weekend, a girl was sitting in the chicken shop looking very dejected. Poor thing had tumbled over in six inch heels and twisted an ankle.

Six or seven inch heels: I would not bother with them unless you have a fetish for stilettos. They only add a marginal bit of definition to your calves. I always think that shorter girls look sexier and more like real girls, so no need to magnify your size if you are already six foot!

Eighth: Stockings.

FORGET ABOUT THESE TOO; they are a bag of trouble. Shave and tan or wear trousers. If you cannot do that...well you may have no choice – but they will not last two minutes without snagging. I wonder if they may provide some cushioning for the shoes, but I doubt it after five hours dancing in a club.

To stocking or not to? It really depends how you see yourself and what you want out of drag and where your ideas lay. You may like the tattered stocking look. "One of my punters ripped 'em"... Many queens do the three stockings and hairy legs, but you will not believe the feeling you get after shaving (the first time can feel a bit strange – you get used to it). Then after tanning and a final sheen with some moisturiser – put on the heels and look at yourself. I challenge the 'butchest geezer' in the world to not feel a little tinge of 'something' when you do that. Shaving is covered in tip number one.

If you are doing drag regularly and your partner knows about it, then why not shave? You can grow it back quick enough if you need to go on holiday or play football. Or pre-tan and go on holiday shaved and highly tanned – if you dare! The tan hides it slightly and looks so good, you will properly confuse people. You can pretend you are a cyclist, as they used to shave for some obscure reason to do with streamlining – or a bodybuilder in competition mode – as they shave. It is amazing what is allowed and not allowed in polite society.

Nine: If you are at 'boy in a dress' stage and you want to go further towards arty-drag here is how to progress.

TAKE YOUR CURRENT LOOK AND EXPAND ON IT by taking a couple of elements of it and making them larger than life or exaggerated. So if you like necklaces, wear ten of them stacked. If you like belts, make a huge one that can be seen a mile away.

> All real girls have a 'beacon' somewhere about them. It is a huge "look, look, look at me". It is only one thing a bit outrageous: a big pom-pom or hat or a huge scarf, skin-tight-tights, shocking green hair, huge earrings, or day-glo pink trainers; even if the rest is very bland. It makes you look; then you may notice other things. Watch them and learn.

Make-up needs to be more exaggerated than the tranny look unless it is immaculate. My make-up was never that fabulous, but most of them were not looking at my face anyway! Kevin Aucoin's classic book, *Making Faces*, is a great start for different themed looks. Just remember what I said re: foundations.

Attention to detail needs to be laboured at – make sure you are clipped and trimmed, no-one really wants to see hairs sticking out of your neckline or your nose; unless we are making some kind of political statement on gender fluidity. Make sure your stuff is clean and does not stink of twenty club-nights. A friend of mine never washed anything and some it stunk!

I use Coco Chanel. It is worth it. People notice it as you waft past or stand at the bar – I have had a lot of compliments on it, it must suit my skin. [On perfumes, make sure you are getting the *eau de parfum* minimum or the pure perfume, it will last for years even though you have to spend £100.]

Get a bigger hat.

Transformer once showed us how to make a simple headdress base: Sculpt some tin-foil over your head and bind the lump together with tape. Once done you can paint with glue and sprinkle glitter dust (large particles) over it or attach whatever else to it (huge feathers are an easy option). Go to professional stage suppliers and buy a few tubs of 'large particle' glitter dust. Most other stuff can come from charity shops/bins/pound-shops. I once covered a builder's hard hat with pink glitter with matching tool belt.

Make giant hoops from light, plastic tubing with a central belt and supporting connecting tabs of fabric (like a wagon wheel). These will make internal shapers for huge outfits and enable you to hang fabric over them and look huge; as they did three-hundred years ago with whale-bones. I have seen dresses with multiple hoops looking like a wedding cake. Miss Thierry was very good at this technique. She ought to write a book about it.

Start by going to dress-up parties and clubs where other dress-ups go. If you are good enough, one day, you will get a tap on the arm, "Hey, we are having a party at ABC, can you come along? We will give you free drinks and VIP passes." That is a good start.

There are many schisms of dress-up. We queens are not really into aping or copying looks (though there are a few Marilyn Monroes about) or doing characters at comic-cons or attending regular fancy dress parties.

Never buy ready-made costumes. This would not make you a true drag-queen, merely a fancy-dress party attendee. You can get a dress-maker to make things for you if you are hopeless with a sewing machine. This will cost more and you cannot quickly alter stuff and re-mould it or adapt it through trial and error; as when you make outfits yourself from scratch and you can re-stitch a seam in seconds.

You need to start thinking creatively and making all your own stuff (or buy base bits and alter them) as you want to look unique. The charity shop pound rail or equivalent at TKMaxx is a good start. Online is tricky with the sizing as you will be a bigger size on top than below, unless you are shaped like a pencil.

Made or altered outfits do not need to be perfectly finished (no-one will inspect the inside stitching in a dark nightclub) but you do not want outfits looking too rough either. They need to 'pass' in club-lighting looking slick.

Mostly, male drag is a feminine pastiche but it can veer more towards 'man-drag-dress-up'; the retired rock star look – you can get away with that more easily and avoid any agro on the bus far more than if you stuff silicones in a dress.

Ten: Some final words (Anything more I can think of).

Check current club rules as some while back Heaven banned high heels. I was stabbed in the foot a few times and it is easy to twist an ankle in big heels.

To get past the door staff, in the early days, before you get backstage privileges, you will have to turn up dressed at the door. Factor in a lot of taxi-fares and local hotels to this. Best is to get a partner to share taxis, provide support and back-up. Make sure you are evenly matched as you do not want to be cringing over your colleague's looks or lack of them, even if you are totally different genres. I am contradicting what I said earlier about freedom of expression, but if you want to look good in drag and get noticed and maybe paid, the above is necessary in my opinion.

The hardest part with partying is getting out and doing it. Once you have a plan it is a lot easier. Make sure you have an escape route: in case things do not pan out as planned! Going out for real is a big, big effort, but once you are standing at that bar, with others of your own type, it is worth it.

See you on Saturday night in the Village!

Postscript: This text was written during the Coronavirus crisis of 2021. Actually getting out to a party again or mincing about in the Village seems a remote prospect. However, things change fast and get back to normal surprisingly quickly, like after a war. You will at least be prepared and waiting in the wings. I have made a couple of new outfits in this time. If you know there is an actual event to attend in the future, that will raise you to action quick enough.

Postscript 2: We are now in 2022, everyone is out again as normal; all the clubs and bars are thumping again and it was worth the wait. Most businesses survived some have changed a bit, sadly Napoleons in Manchester shut down, which was tranny heaven.

See over pages for diagrams and pictures.

Appendices

1

It is interesting to muse on the creation and then the deletion of Bohemian areas and 'gay villages' in city centres. Camden Town (once, a Mecca for vintage gear) is suffering the same fate as Soho in terms of re-development. Bohemian centres or gay villages for business or pleasure, form themselves naturally in slightly run-down or non-trendy areas, which, however, have some charm about them; having cobbled streets or older or former disused commercial buildings. The rents are cheap, and artists, creatives, gay/bi-sexual and sub-cult people are attracted to this small area or street for business and pleasure (unlike the purpose-made 'artisan studios' for rent in a converted tobacco warehouses or the like).

Canal Street, Manchester, is a great example of organic re-use within former commercial buildings (presumably serving the canal's trade). Eventually, when the sub-cult venues, flea markets or squatters that move in to the run-down premises become above board and legit and legal, the bigger operators move in and shish it all up a few notches and then the street or quadrant starts to become popular with the mainstream population and becomes a destination. When gay centres develop (Soho was never a purely gay centre or village; it was very mixed but with a good handful of gay venues: above and below board), they usually become very vibrant if they consist of clubs and bars that are attractive and open to the street (unlike secret clubs where you knock three times). For some reason straight or non-sub-cult people simply have to go to the area now: In Canal Street at night, there are usually quite a few groups of girls out on hen-nights (the blokes are a bit embarrassed to be seen there for stag nights which is why there are no lads).

Although straight people have hundreds of bars and clubs of their own in other parts of town, somehow a gay village or street which has a few gay venues is always better for them. The theory that the straight girls (who like the gay areas) feel less bothered by rutting males is, I think, a red-herring. Canal Street (designated a gay village on all official maps) has turned into a hen-night parade in the evenings. Surely there are other places they could go?

When you walk down Canal Street at night, hen-girls pass you and their body-language does not have that: "Hi, we are visiting and in your space tonight, thanks for letting us in" tone. It is more like: "Hey you, out of my way; we are going to take over this space and you are a minor annoyance in the process". I think this is some sort of natural, ESP-communicated thought process that straight/normal/non-sub-cult people use to take over and 'clean up' an area or venue that serves sub-cult people, not like themselves, and then claim it as their own. Advanced warfare via, tiaras, tutus and huge pink angel wings? This is the same as 'textiles' frequenting nudist beaches and making the nudists feel like the outsiders in the one area they have earmarked for themselves to feel comfortable in. I used to see them walking up and down aside Brighton nudist beach, fully clothed, when they had miles of normal beach just adjacent.

Canal Street, Manchester, has had a chequered history over the decades. In recent history, bouncers in gay venues were not admitting people whom they suspected were not gay which was causing quite a ruckus. Firstly, sexuality is very difficult to prove, with all the grey areas included that become apparent: Take a bi-sexual who is out with his female partner. The female may also have relationships with other women, how do you prove any of that? This door selection can be understood if straight people (or non-Bohemian types) are polluting or watering down a small sub-cult establishment: it could be argued that "If you are straight, why do you need to patronise a gay bar; there are a thousand straight bars (or normal establishments) right round the corner, just for you; we only have this one, and why should you spoil it?" It is difficult unless it is a private club.

On the other hand, gay culture is self-diluting as many gay folk (and trans people) like to frequent normal venues and not be segregated or stigmatised. However, even if this is the trend, it is nice to know that there are still places to go, 'for people like me' and why should 'other types' make us feel uncomfortable there.

Nothing is that simple and some may object on principles of freedom and non-discrimination both ways. But would a non-Jew be allowed to attend a Jewish school? Would there be any point or need for that? If women can have rural institutes and 'women only clubs and female-only gyms or classes' (no objection from me on that) then why can't men have their own clubs, segments or facilities if they choose to? I wonder if Studio 54 would contravene non-discrimination rules now... "they didn't let me in because my outfit was not outrageous enough".

As all the cutesy, cobbled Victorian and Edwardian industrial areas of all our cities are now firmly 'post-Bohemia', I wonder if a new Bohemia will regenerate in the outer suburbs within down-at-heel or unfashionable shopping malls or 1930s shop fronted streets surrounded by semi-detached housing? Regarding Manchester, the Northern Quarter, which does not seem overly busy when I was around there in the daytime, would make a great, new village...

2

Once in a club, any coats are put in the bag-room, then the fun: to start exploring. Some clubs are cavernous and it is part of the thrill to wander about and get a bit lost in the dark maze and get nabbed by someone and thoroughly 'seen to'. Fetish clubs are usually well-equipped with very expensive gear: stocks, crosses, racks and all kinds of slings and accessories –

if you like all that. Rooms can be themed (one club now even has cars inside to replicate a dogging site). Some parts are for groups or couples only depending on the day or time. Some areas inside are lit and some are in total blackout. Go where you want and do what you like (so long as the other party consent). Many have bars and you can get food and drink and some are very sociable (this also applies to swingers' clubs where there is a lot of crossover). Some fetish clubs insist on leather or rubber, some are more flexible; and it depends on the night; TVs are usually welcome and considered fine if simply dressed, but read the flyer first in case it is strictly rubber or leather. The big parties are usually all-sorts and one-offs. You do not need to adhere to the themed dress code on the flyer unless it says 'strictly'. You will need to arrive dressed to most of them, to show you are in 'fetish' mode unless they have changing and you get there early. Many tranny or swingers' clubs, which have regular weekly nights (or days) have changing rooms and showers, which makes it very easy for trannies.

3

Leeds Pride was great day. The whole town was bedecked in flags. Thousands of people were lining the route. But for townspeople and business it is any excuse for a festival and promotion. So for one day LGBTQ+ rainbow flags are everywhere. There was a chance missed for some rallying speeches, or even the local MP to say something positive on a stage that everyone could hear. I was around all day and did not hear of any such thing. It has turned into a big town festival, people standing around and drinking, too many 'permissions' are needed for everything, there is little spontaneity anywhere and it is totally invaded by straights who always want to take over anything gay. There was a special event in the park, but you have to pay for that, which will exclude many.

Making rouleau strapping

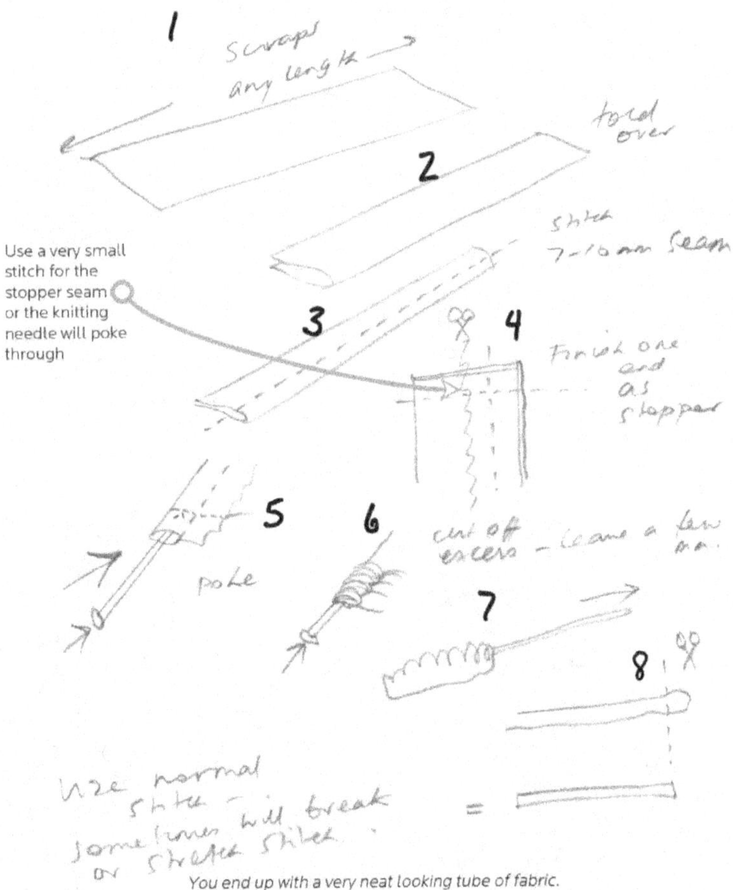

You end up with a very neat looking tube of fabric, about 5-10mm wide. Perfect for anything, including alterations and extra straps to keep things in place. Use it for making a gaff, bikinis, bra-tops, bag-straps.

The tricky bit is turning the stitched rectangle inside out, hence the stopper seam as shown. Use a knitting needle, and keep pushing inside out, gently until you can pull it and it all goes through on the needle. Cut the end bobble off afterwards. If you find any holes where stitching has broken you can still use it or you may need to make a new piece. Always make loads extra. In lycra, it will take a fair pull if you use a medium stitch – expect some stitches to pop here and there though.

Making The gaff ✂

Here are some basic instructions on how to make this fabled garment. You will have to experiment a lot. Start with buying a one meter length of heavy-weight lycra. That will give you enough fabric, as you will cut loads out before you perfect it.
T.E.= Trial and error.

Make a couple of metres of rouleau spaghetti strapping and a thong-shape as shown, from the fabric.

Place the thong shape over you in front of the mirror. Allowing for balls to be tucked in, it should hang down and tuck up behind inbetween your cheeks. Do not make the back too long. Part of the engineering is that you can pull it tightly from front to back. You can stitch the front of the thong part to the strap at this point, just with a light, tack-stitch.

Stitch on the strapping and T.E. the lengths. You can make a bow on the sides (then stitch down later if you want, for a decorative effect) or join with a eye and a half hitch or slipped hitch knot each side, so you can adjust or re-adjust it at any point easily. It can be a bit of a handful to get it all in place and tie up, but practise.

You can elasticate the sides of the thong piece, though it will lay flatter with just a side seam for strength and rigidity.

Attach the piece to the strap either flat on with a row of stitching or do a neater turned over hem front and rear. You could use a tubed seam to pass the strap through, but in wearing, the thong will rouche up in the middle.

The sides of the thong bit do not need to be elasticated. A seam is needed here to keep it all taut. I have sometimes not bothered with that. If you elasticate the sides, it will be more of a standard pair of briefs and you will get much more of a bulge out front. You can make an elasticated one for when wearing loose stuff, not body hugging outfits, for which this is intended.

After T.E. and cutting out about six of these, you will be refining the shape to fit your own body and size. Once the side straps are nice and tight and the thong the right shape, practise.

Put on, then with a smooth all-in-one action, push your balls in and back (they can go into the cavities, make sure you are not in any pain though). At the same time, flatten your cock down and under a bit. Again, do this only if it is comfortable. Pull the back of the thong tight up and back; your front should look farily flat now. The straps should be snug enough around your waist to keep all in place for hours. You should re-adjust and check frequently. If your balls pop out (an Inbetweener's moment), then the thong part needs to be a few mm wider. The increments are small between success and failure. Make sure all your balls are tucked in neatly and no bits showing. This is for underclothing really, but if you make it smartly, you can use as outerwear...as I have done.

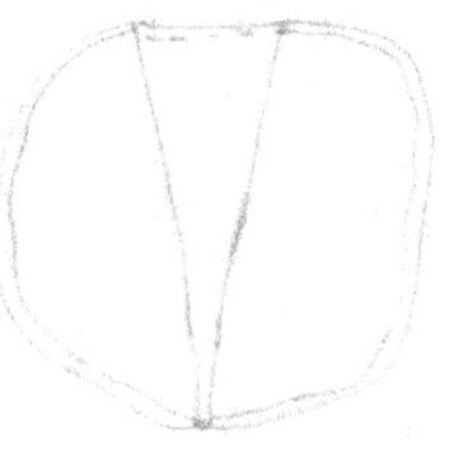

Tracy Tramp

TRACY TRAMP was born in London in 1967. In July 1969 the U.S.A. Eagle Rover landed on the surface of the moon. Millions around the world watched the whole thing on TV, in the latest technicolour, apart from us as we had no telly. The Rover lifted off the surface to re-join the mother-ship, ship fifty miles above. 'Man's first step' left the first pile of litter on the surface of another world that had been undisturbed for a billion years.

TT's northwest London Jewish bubble of life hinged around family, bar-mitzvahs and (luckily) getting into J.F.S school – at the old Camden Road site. The alternatives at the time were too horrific to be contemplated. It was a statement of fact that at John Kelly (comprehensive) School, heads *would* be stuffed down toilets.

Childhood was a happy time for the many kids in the Edwardian terraces near Gladstone Park. Silver Jubilee party, 1977; Raleigh Choppers; hot, steamy summers and letters typed on manual typewriters. The Krays had been away for over ten years already; lots of people were wandering about who had fought in or survived the war; red phone boxes ate 2p pieces for a call. TT was kitted out in purple flares, paisley shirts and sported a Jimmy Hendrix style huge mop of black curls.

Then the digital age stealthily crept in (little did they know) with hand-held space invader games, digital watches and Atari games. Kids with red hair and freckles would programme on a 'blue screen', while other kids were wasting time reading comics and playing in dangerous adventure playgrounds (with no matting). Alan Sugar was building his business empire from a market stall (or so he said).

Friends were in and out of the house; cricket was played in the street and in the park and cycling was around suburban London (with no helmets – and we all survived). By the late 70s, many family members of TT had moved out of the inner zones; the great Jewish northwest migration; to the more exclusive feeding grounds of Stanmore and Pinner.

In the grand cycle of the neighbourhood rise and fall: palace to slum and back to palace again; the much-loved mahogany newel post, panelled doors and tiled hallways of the speculative Edwardian builders were not enough to stop family and TT from adventuring further abroad. The 1980s were a time when everyone wanted more. Willesden High Road was not enough; and the neighbourhood *was* getting a bit rough around the edges. TT's school-friends in London, soon to be rudely abandoned for better prospects, prophesied grief and punishment. The mahogany newel post, which had seen countless family events and eyeballed guests arriving for lunch and dinner parties, for at least two decades, was left to greet new owners.

The move to Dockenfield, Surrey, heralded the start of a life of contrasts. The detached house bordered the Alice Holt Forest and the county boundary ran through a rivulet in the grounds – in which the huge removal lorry became lodged fast after taking a short cut through the front meadow.

TT was kitted out with rugby shorts, flannels, labelled shirts, a blazer and a (gorgeous) tweed jacket, from Elphicks of Farnham – the requitals of an attractive looking boarding school (housed in a huge Jacobethan mansion built by a captain of hops) in an idyllic location by the River Wey, at Frensham and a cross-country-run from Frensham Ponds.

The extensive half-timbered exterior: circled by lush lawns, protected by its ha-ha – and beyond that, the playing fields and finally the road that led to genteel Farnham – hid a tougher and slightly bitter inner: a life of wedgies, cold baths, forced rugby and penalty drill. The CCF including the army cadets – the prime focus of the school (bar rugby), provided a welcome diversion for TT. After a lucky chance, playing the jester, and impressing top-brass, TT was immediately made up to Lance-Corporal (and permanent) duty NCO (avoiding the formal exams) and allowed to wear a huge red sash on parade. With 'immediate effect' TT could now strut about all day in uniform on CCF day, promising punishments for petty offences to contemporaries: the sons of the great and the good of Surrey and the Hong Kong elites – who wielded big power on normal days but had not quite passed their NCO exams yet.

A smoking habit, and constant convictions for it, halted any other advancement in school honours and this disgrace was mercifully cut short by entry to a sixth form college back in London and progression in favoured subjects such as graphics.

After Watford College of Printing and then the London College of Printing (enrolled on the legendary Typo-Design course), TT decided to fulfil academic desires and to polish a long interest in the history – and especially in the languages of the ancient Near East – and applied to study Assyriology at SOAS. 'Ancient Near Eastern Studies' was the most unique and a highly respected course at this former 'school for spies' in Russell Square. Conversations in Arabic and Chinese echoed around its corridors of excellence.

Most of the time was spent in marbled and chromed vaults of knowledge: the magnificent libraries of SOAS and UCL; thumbing through Assyrian dictionaries, periodicals and lexicons of cuneiform characters, compiled by Babylonian scribal students. TT had already mastered the Akkadian construct-genitive before enrolling – and at the end of the first year achieved top marks.

An unrivalled fusion of tuition from academic nobility, slick early twentieth century architecture and Georgian squares housing many research 'institutes' (a filing cabinet in a room) was bathed in the perpetual and stern gaze of the (even slicker) university HQ; the unrivalled glory of Senate House; a stepped tower that reached to the sky. It secreted away even more libraries, greater opulence and a breakfast in its swishy canteen. This was many a foreign dictators' dream HQ for London – and the building, a fraction of its' original intention, emitted an uplifting aura of academic hope and aspiration for life. The SOAS student bar had not yet been taken over by Costa (fortune) and the sticky carpets soaked up earnest discussions over Sumerian grammar and other ribald subjects. TT managed to get lunch in the SOAS canteen for .45p: plate of rice, free gravy and a glass of water.

TT had, by this time, unfortunately, become immersed in the addictive, time-consuming, self-destructive and narcissistic world of the London clubbing and dress-up scene. The only other lifelong activity which sustained any remaining unspent energies was climbing and mountaineering: a wholesome contrast to the world of glamorous celebrity parties, club-life and the debauchery of the T-girl clubs.

The future now holds out well for TT, staring back at her wrinkled reflection from a cracked mirror in a dingy apartment in an outer suburb and leaving faded old press-cuttings and mentions in gossip columns on the sideboard; that the rare visitor may glance at and return a nod of bemused approval.

Brighton, nightclub party. Must have been a 'beach theme'. *Unknown photographer.*

The whole gang of us. 'The Freaks'.
[x], Fabio, [x], Transformer, K, TT, Miss T, [x], Candy Bar